FORD, Arthur M. Political economics of rural poverty in the South.
  Ballinger, 1973. 101p tab bibl 73-11148. 10.00. ISBN
  0-88410-005-7. C.I.P.
A revision of economist Ford's dissertation, arguing that, in the Deep
South and Appalachia since the mid-'30s, government agricultural subsidies have primarily benefited large commercial farmers, who have
been able to integrate new capital and technology into their operations, thereby displacing large numbers of low-skilled workers. These
workers are largely unable to find employment because the major
growth in employment has been in the service sector of the economy,
for which they are unqualified. Ford presents this argument, and
statistical data to support it, supplemented by discussions of economic
and noneconomic definitions of poverty, the culture-of-poverty thesis,
and the adequacy of neoclassical economic theory and Keynesian analysis to explain rural poverty and prescribe solutions for unemployment
resulting from agricultural displacement. He argues that this agrarian
transformation took place as a result of political intervention, rather
than market effects but only very sketchily outlines the way in which
this political influence was exercised. Bibliography; index. Some minor
errors. For advanced undergraduate and graduate students.

**Political Economics
of Rural Poverty
in the South**

Political Economics of Rural Poverty in the South

Arthur M. Ford
Southern Illinois University

1 0 0 4 7 0

Ballinger Publishing Company • Cambridge, Mass.
A Subsidiary of J.B. Lippincott Company

Library of Congress Catalog Card Number 73-11148

International Standard Book Number 0-88410-005-7

Printed in the United States of America

Library of Congress Cataloging in Publication Data
Ford, Arthur M
    Political economics of rural poverty in the South.
    Bibliography: p.
    1. Rural poor—Southern States. 2. Southern States—Economic conditions—
1818- 3. Southern States—Rural conditions. I. Title.
HC107.A133P615   330.9'75   73-11148
ISBN 0-88410-005-7

For
Marie and Sheldon Weaver,
Vernie Ford,
and the late Rawleigh M. Ford

Contents

List of Tables

Preface

The fundamental premise of this book is that the study of poverty should be a study of inequality. Therefore, the task of eliminating poverty requires that one determine the causes of inequality. However, in reviewing the literature on poverty, one is struck by the general absence of any systematic attempt to inquire into cause itself and/or the general inference that the cause is individual failure. The methodology that has gained general acceptance in studies of poverty is oriented toward identifying the poor, not toward seeking the reason for their condition. First, the attempt to define some objective measure of poverty not only avoids the whole question of income distribution but is a value-laden measure in its own right. Second, the innumerable studies of the personal characteristics of the poor have led to confusion between attributes of poverty and their causes. The whole approach to date has been to treat poverty as a distinctive phenomenon to be studied in micro terms rather than as a distribution problem related to social structure in society as a whole.

Where there has been some concern with causes of poverty, a "cultural deviation" thesis has generally been advanced as an explanation. Since the "culture of poverty" thesis studies have failed to distinguish between expectations, aspirations, behavior, and values, cause and effect have been obscured. The findings of this study indicate that there is strong reason to believe that cultural deviance is the result of adaptation to deprivation; it is not the cause of poverty. The fundamental mistake that authors of culture of poverty studies make is to observe behavioral patterns associated with negative expectations and conclude that they are observing distinctive cultural values producing different aspirations.

In other words, it is argued here that rural poverty cannot be understood except within the context of social change for society as a whole. In this context then, Chapters 2 and 3 outline the major characteristics of the agrarian revolution experienced by the South, specifically the Core South and Appalachia, since the mid-thirties. The essential findings are that the consequences of government subsidy during this period reduced the cost of capital relative to labor, resulting in massive capitalization of farming operations in the South. Because of the upper income farmer's ability to exercise control over government subsidy in his own interest, the consequence of the agricultural transformation was a rather sudden release of large quantities of low-skilled labor seeking employment in the nonagricultural sector. However, communities and/or regions do not have an unlimited ability to absorb large amounts of unskilled labor at a given point in time. The alternatives for that proportion of unskilled labor unable to find employment in the nonagricultural sector are reduced to two: remain in the region at a reduced level of living or migrate.

Chapter 4 discusses the perverse effects of a selective migration pattern as experienced by Appalachia and the Core South. The findings indicate clearly that these areas are net losers economically because their better-trained young people move out, leaving behind an aging and lower-skilled population unable to finance those improvements in the public sector which are necessary to turn the region around from its present declining economic position. Further, recent data indicates that structural transformation in the nonagricultural sector, the rise of the service economy, has limited the employment opportunities for low-skilled labor in the nonagricultural sector. Initial studies of migration, such as the one done by Hathaway, have found that 40 percent of those who migrated have lower incomes in the nonagricultural sector than in their last year in agriculture. These findings suggest that labor market reallocation of redundant labor has led to an increase rather than a decrease in the disparity in the distribution of income.

The final argument of Chapter 4 calls attention to the fact that the findings concerning structural transformation in the South are rather contrary to what modern neoclassical economics would lead one to expect. Further, this evidence would lead one to suspect that the current neoclassical paradigm may be a special case with limited applicability in explaining how our present system operates. The problem with the current neoclassical paradigm, as has been pointed out by the Cambridge Critics, is that modern neoclassical theorists have assumed an a priori structure of production for which the neoclassical results hold when in fact there may exist structures of production in which the relations do not hold. Consequently, where structures do not hold, the distribution of income cannot be explained in terms of marginal productivity theory nor can low-wage poverty be explained in terms of market efficiency. In other words, once one drops the a priori assumptions regarding structure, it is quite possible to conceive of a socioeconomic transformation that has differential impact on the various classes of society. To understand this kind of structural transformation, one needs to know about such matters as corporate power structures, unions, structure of industry, politics, and ways in which structural transformation is filtered through a social system. All of this suggests the necessity of a new paradigm which begins by coming to grips with the nature and use of power.

Arthur M. Ford
Carbondale
March 1973

Acknowledgments

In my study of rural poverty I have received assistance from a number of individuals. Byron Bunger and Peter Anthony served willingly as sounding boards and made valuable suggestions as I struggled with various troublesome passages. John Owen, Edward Nell, and David Schwartzman all criticized the manuscript, forcing me to tighten up, qualify, and/or rethink certain aspects of the study when it was being prepared as a doctoral thesis at the Graduate Faculty of Political and Social Science of the New School for Social Research. Robert L. Heilbroner deserves special thanks for the care he expended on the entire manuscript, making many valuable suggestions with regard to both content and style. He has, to borrow an expression from Doug Dowd, truly mastered the art of "criticism with love," a rarity in our egocentric profession. Last, a special thanks goes to my wife, Ramona, who assisted in both sociological commentary and editing. Needless to say, I take sole responsibility for the contents of this study and the views expressed are not necessarily shared by those with whom I have worked.

Introduction

In the late medieval era (Keynes' *General Theory* had just appeared) when
I first studied economics, there existed a quaint area called Agricultural
Economics, along with some other odd fields called Regulation of Public Utili-
ties, Economics of Transportation, and the like. Then the *General Theory*
bloomed, and under the dazzling illumination of macro-economics those old-
fashioned subjects retreated into the background. Who wanted to study crops,
after all, when the Propensity to Consume offered such Olympian prospects?
Agricultural Economics more or less disappeared from the scene.

Today, along with some of the other medieval fields of economics,
agricultural economics is enjoying a long overdue revival; and Professor Ford's
book is a welcome sign that agriculture will again receive its due recognition.
The reasons for this revival are worth noting. First, macro-economics, despite
its truly brilliant light, has proved a disappointing tool for dealing with problems such as rural poverty (or the control of corporations, etc.). Hence interest
is turning again to the use of economics as a means for lighting up specific
areas that one cannot investigate from Mount Olympus. Second, we have become aware that for all the talk of a Post-Industrial Society, men must still
eat; and that eating is not a matter to be taken for granted in a world that seems
determined to make Malthus come true. And last, we have begun to realize that
the great exodus out of agriculture that lay at the base of so many social problems of recent decades is by no means over. There remain some 1,466,000
American farmers with a farm income of less than $2,500 (although many of
them may work in local industry), and the influx of machinery and organization that has forced out the small farmer over the last half century can still
push several million blacks and whites (when families are included) from rural
into urban squalor.

Perhaps the first two reasons for the revival of interest in agricultural economics are the more fundamental; but in terms of America's next decade, I suspect the third reason is the most pressing. With our urban centers already in a state of acute disrepair, we can hardly face with equanimity the prospect of another mass migration of ill-equipped displaced rural workers. Yet, if the technological and organizational possibilities already at hand are fully utilized, it will take only about 100,000 large, highly capitalized incorporated farms to turn out the food we will need; and this will "free" between a million and two million workers to seek their "fortunes" in the big city.

This prospect is a grim one. Only well-planned and active social policies can prevent a repetition of the disastrous rural emigration of the 1950s and 1960s. Unfortunately, it is also possible that policies launched in the name of "saving" the small farmer will in fact be used to accelerate his displacement. In short, the drama described in the pages of this book may be replayed again.

Ford does not focus his study on the future, but on the past. However, the lessons he draws from his political/economic analysis are all too easily applicable to the years ahead. All one can say is that forewarned is forearmed. One may be doubtful—as I am—that we will use the warning to avert a repetition of the past, but at least we can no longer claim, after this book, that we did not understand how technology "works" when it enters the agricultural sector, or how political elements can turn a program of good intentions into one of outrageous results.

Political Economics of Rural Poverty in the South is a welcome book that has much to teach us—provided, of course, that we are willing to learn.

Robert L. Heilbroner
New York
March 1973

Political Economics
of Rural Poverty
in the South

Chapter One

Rural Poverty: A General Overview

The process of social recognition is always a slow affair, and this has certainly been the case in recognizing the fact of poverty. In 1940 the Roosevelt Administration conducted a hearing on rural poverty. Thereafter, except for a Senate hearing in 1947 and a flurry of political debates surrounding the welfare aspects of the Agriculture Adjustment Act (AAA), rural poverty generally disappeared from consideration until the early 1960s when Michael Harrington [1962, p. 43] labeled rural poverty as the "harshest and most bitter poverty" in existence. The general reaction to Harrington's statement was surprise or disbelief. How could there be any rural poor? Had not agriculture been favorably treated by various government policies since the thirties? Were we not talking about the shiftless few who refused to work?

At about the same time as Harrington's *Other America* came Harry Caudill's *Night Comes to the Cumberlands* and Thomas R. Ford's *The Southern Appalachian Region: A Survey*, both indicating serious trouble in Appalachia. In that same period, the civil rights movement started to gain momentum, and news coverage began to offer occasional glimpses of the nature of black rural poverty in the deep South. Finally, in 1967, twenty-seven years after the Roosevelt hearings, came a second Presidential Commission whose findings finally permit an accurate assessment of the nature and scope of rural poverty in "modern times" [U.S. President 1968].

At the time Harrington was writing, there were approximately 9.6 million poor rural families and 6.3 million poor unattached rural individuals. Of this number, 4.5 million poor families and 2.0 million poor individuals lived in the South (see Table 1-1) [Kain and Persky 1968].

Table 1-1. Number of Families with Income Below $3,000 and Unrelated Individuals with Income Below $1,500, by Residence and Race: 1960

Residence	South		Rest of U.S.		Entire U.S.		
	White	*Nonwhite*	*White*	*Nonwhite*	*White*	*Nonwhite*	*Total*
Families:							
Urban	1,230	764	2,720	513	3,950	1,277	5,227
Rural farm	606	223	729	11	1,335	234	1,569
Rural nonfarm	1,176	470	1,153	53	2,329	524	2,853
Total	3,013	1,458	4,602	577	7,615	2,035	9,650
Unrelated individuals	1,456	559	3,892	416	5,347	976	6,323

Source: Kain and Persky, 1968, p. 306.

In national terms, the South had 30 percent of all families but 46 percent of all poor families, and 27 percent of all individuals but 32 percent of all poor individuals (see Table 1-2). With respect to the categories of rural poor, the South had 12 percent of all rural families but 26 percent of the rural poor. Perhaps most surprising is the statistic on race: approximately two-thirds of the Southern poor were white (see Table 1-3).

An up-dating of the rural poor as of March 1965 (see Table 1-4), using a modified Social Security definition of poverty, does not significantly alter the picture [U.S. President 1967]. Rural America as of that date comprised roughly 30 percent of the total population, but it numbered 40 percent of the poor. While poor whites still outnumbered poor blacks in absolute terms, the incidence of poverty among blacks was a shocking 78 percent [Kain and Persky 1968]. In short, rural poverty was significant as a form of poverty, and it was concentrated in the South. This condition, with only small changes, continues to the present day.

Because of the overall heterogeneity of the larger region, it is useful to disaggregate the South into two fairly homogenous subregions—the deep South or "Core South" and Appalachia.[1] The distinguishing characteristics of such a division are important. The Core South emerged in the thirties with a predominantly agrarian economy—indeed it is still characterized by its cotton plantations. In addition, it had a major concentration of blacks in its population (see Table 1-5).

Appalachia, in contrast, has had a higher percentage of nonagricultural employment—32 percent as against 24 percent. In addition, its agricultural sector is characterized by mixed family farming rather than plantation farming and has a significantly smaller black population—16 percent as against 32 percent. In short, rural poverty takes the form of being primarily black poverty in the Core South and white poverty in Appalachia. This distinction is made to determine, to the extent that data permits, the differential impact of agrarian change on rural whites and blacks in the South.

DEFINITION OF POVERTY

Any study of poverty must come to grips with alternative definitions of poverty. More detailed definitions have been given subsequent to Harrington's relatively unsophisticated definition of an annual income of $3,000 for family and

1. The Core South is defined to include South Carolina, Georgia, Alabama, Mississippi, Arkansas, and Louisiana. Southern Appalachia includes Virginia, West Virginia, North Carolina, Kentucky, and Tennessee.

Table 1-2. Families with Income Below $3,000 and Unrelated Individuals with Incomes Below $1,500 as a Percent of All Poor Families and Unrelated Individuals, by Race and Residence: 1960

Residence	South		Rest of U.S.		Entire U.S.		
	White	Nonwhite	White	Nonwhite	White	Nonwhite	Total
Families:							
Urban	12.7	7.9	28.2	5.3	40.9	13.2	54.1
Rural farm	6.3	2.3	7.6	0.1	13.8	2.4	16.2
Rural nonfarm	12.2	4.9	11.9	0.5	24.1	5.4	29.5
Total	31.2	15.1	47.7	6.0	78.9	21.1	100.0
Unrelated individuals	23.0	8.8	61.5	6.6	84.6	15.4	100.0

Source: Kain and Persky, 1968, p. 306.

Table 1-3. Families and Unrelated Individuals by Residence and Race as a Percent of All U.S. Families and Unrelated Individuals: 1960

Residence	South		Rest of U.S.		Entire U.S.		
	White	Nonwhite	White	Nonwhite	White	Nonwhite	Total
Families:							
Urban	14.8	3.2	48.9	4.0	63.6	7.2	70.8
Rural farm	2.6	0.6	4.2	0.0	6.8	0.6	7.4
Rural nonfarm	7.5	1.4	12.7	0.3	20.2	1.7	21.9
Total	24.9	5.2	65.8	4.3	90.5	9.5	100.0
Unrelated individuals	21.1	6.2	65.6	7.1	86.7	13.3	100.0

Source: Kain and Persky, 1968, p. 306.

Table 1-4. **Number and Distribution of Poor Persons in the U.S.: 1965**

Item	Persons at All Income Levels		Poor Persons		
	Number (mil.)	*Percent (dist.)*	*Number (mil.)*	*Percent (dist.)*	*Percent poor*
U.S.A.	189.9	100.0	44.7	100.0	17.7
Total urban	134.6	70.9	19.9	59.1	14.8
Total rural	55.3	29.1	13.8	40.9	25.0
Farm	13.3	7.0	3.9	11.6	29.3
Nonfarm	42.0	22.1	9.9	29.4	23.6

Source: U.S. President. President's National Advisory Commission on Rural Poverty, 1967, p. 3.

Table 1-5. **Selected Characteristics of the Southern Subregions: 1960**

	Population	*% Black*	*% in Agri.*	*% in Mfg.*	*1950–1960 Net-Migration*
Appalachia	16,989,000	16.6	13.2	31.9	–1,434,300
Core South	16,813,000	31.3	11.8	23.7	–1,719,300

Source: Adapted from Kain and Persky, 1968, p. 290.

$1,500 for unattached individuals. Walter Heller has suggested a minimum of $1,500 for each individual plus $500 for each additional individual up to $4,500. Others have defined poverty as that income level below which no income tax is paid, and a nutritional inadequacy definition has been supplied by the Social Security Administration [Orshansky 1968]. These definitions may be applied uniformly to all sectors of society or they may contain a rural-urban differential.

Orshansky has compared all four of the above definitions and notes that the primary effect of changing the definition of poverty is to change the composition of the poor rather than their absolute number [Ibid.]. For example, using a uniform $3,000 definition, one gets a poverty profile that includes larger numbers of rural poor and aged. Using the Social Security Administration (SSA) definition with a rural-urban differential, the profile changes to include more nonfarm families and children. For example, under the Harrington definition there would be 33.4 million poor—one out of seven a farm resident, and one out of three a child under eighteen years of age. Under a modified SSA definition, there would be 34.6 million poor, but the number of poor children would be one million higher, and the farm poor would drop to one out of eleven.

Which is correct? As Orshansky notes, government policy aimed at a profile of farm and aged poor clearly cannot serve the needs of nonfarm families and poor children. She places her preference with the SSA definition. A number of recent studies of poverty have used the SSA definition, such as the National Advisory Commission on Rural Poverty's 1967 report (see Table 1-4), suggesting a general shift of opinion in that direction.

The SSA procedure is to define a necessary minimum caloric intake, to estimate the proportion of the family budget spent on food, and to derive an Engels coefficient from the actual food expenditure which is then used to establish an estimate of the minimum income necessary to provide adequate nutritional needs [Ibid.] [2] Rural poverty is then calculated with a differential ranging from 70 to 85 percent of the urban cutoff.

There is, however, good reason to believe that the SSA definition, as well as the others mentioned, are not adequate definitions of rural poverty. In essence, any subsistence definition of poverty is relative and ignores certain relevant aspects of poverty. As Miller [1971] has noted:

> The essential fallacy of a fixed poverty line is that it fails to recognize the relative nature of "needs." The poor will not be satisfied with a given level of living year after year when the levels of those around them are going up at the rate of about 3 percent per year. [P. 120]

This criticism has been advanced by Martin Rein [1968]. His critique of the SSA definition of poverty as an objective, absolute measure has three points of attack. First, he objects to a definition of poverty in terms of subsistence rather than in terms of income inequality or social externality.[3] His objection is that a definition of poverty as an income inadequate to acquire the necessities of life based on an income-food expenditure relationship ignores noneconomic aspects of poverty and the general issue of distribution of income. Second, Rein points out that the technique of estimating the cutoff point for poverty is arbitrary even if one accepts the SSA subsistence definition. One can define a minimum caloric intake based upon soybeans that is exceedingly low in cost. But it should be obvious that any such diet involves some expert's judgment of minimum necessary calories, selection among foods, assessment of customary eating patterns, as well as various assumptions as to the economic behavior of the poor. The issue was clearly dramatized by George Orwell in his description of

---

2. See also Rein, [1968, pp. 116-130] and Miller [1971, pp. 117-123].

3. Rein defines *inequality* as being "concerned with the relative position of income groups to each other" whereas *externality* concerns itself with the "social consequences of poverty on the rest of society rather than in terms of the needs of the poor."

unemployed Welsh coal miners. Orwell noted that a good portion of their limited income was spent on either nonfood items such as tobacco and alcohol, or on luxury food items such as chocolate and expensive tea.

> Would it not be better if they spent more money on wholesome things like oranges and whole meal bread or . . . saved on fuel and ate their carrots raw? Yes, it would, but the point is that no ordinary human being is ever going to do such a thing. . . . When you are unemployed, which is to say when you are underfed, harrassed, bored and miserable, you don't want to eat dull wholesome food, you want something a little bit "tasty." [1961, p. 88]

Finally, Rein points out that the size of the Engels coefficient used in the SSA definition is both crucial and arbitrary. To arrive at the cutoff point for poverty it is necessary to estimate an Engels coefficient in order to determine "normal" income-food expenditure relationships. The coefficient commonly used is .33, based upon a 1955 Department of Agriculture survey of the proportion of total family income spent on food by the low income family [Orshansky 1968]. In other words, income must be three times the cost of food. Yet, the Bureau of Labor Statistics in a survey undertaken in 1960–61 estimated the coefficient to be approximately .25 [Ibid.].[4] This would suggest that the cost of food budget should be multiplied by four, rather than three, resulting in a considerably higher cutoff point for defining poverty.

What is important here is that the number of poor is significantly altered by simply changing the size of the Engels coefficient. The higher the coefficient, the lower the cutoff point, and consequently the fewer the poor. For example, Rein [1968] noted that Haber [1966], using a lower coefficient and gross income rather than net income, significantly increases the number of the poor while Friedman [1965], using estimates based on actual consumption and a higher coefficient, cuts poverty in half. Rein's final comments are noteworthy:

> Almost every procedure in the subsistence level definition of poverty can be reasonably challenged. The estimates are based on the consumption patterns of the entire low-income third instead of subgroups of this population. The estimate of nutritional needs take age and sex into account but not physical activity. Average price and average cost are used as the standard for constructing the low cost food plan, rather than actual behavior. . . . We must conclude that subsistence measures of poverty cannot claim to rest solely on a techni-

4. See also Rein, [1968, p. 124].

cal or scientific definition or nutritional adequacy. Values, prefer-
ences and political realities influence the definition of subsistence.
Yet once a biological definition is abandoned and actual consumption is taken into account no absolute measurement of poverty in
subsistence terms is possible. The other conceptions of poverty (inequality and externality) deserve more attention. [P. 130]

In the absence of an agreed-upon definition of poverty and the
resulting variety of definitions used in the studies included here, I will
specify the definition in use at each point and, where possible, compare
these results with other studies using alternative definitions. Although it is
the intent of this study to approach poverty in terms of relative inequality,
the above caveat as to the unavoidable arbitrariness of definitions should be kept
in mind at all times.

NONECONOMIC DIMENSIONS OF POVERTY

There is a tendency for many poverty studies to note noneconomic aspects of
poverty and then to analyze poverty solely in economic terms. Such research
bias is not so much the product of deliberate intent on the part of the economist as it is a reflection on the extreme difficulty in formulating and quantify-
ing the noneconomic aspects of poverty. Yet the mounting literature on "folk
culture" or "culture of poverty" makes it clear that wholly "economic" definitions are inadequate. In studies of rural America, ranging from Agee and Evan's
[1939] 1930's classic, through the work of Caudill [1962] and Weller [1965]
in the 1960s, to Dunbar [1971] in 1970s, there runs a consistent characteriza-
tion of a rural poverty life style that is different from that of urban, nonpoor,
middle-class America. As the President's National Advisory Commission on
Rural Poverty stated, "The poor think differently; they have a different set of
values" [1967, p. 8]. Where there are areas of disagreement and differences in
emphasis as to the content of the life style of the rural poor, common to all is
a society characterized by individualism, fundamentalism, fatalism, traditionalism, familism, anxiety, and a general absence of long-range planning. This "folk
culture" or "culture of poverty" has been exceedingly perplexing to the observer of poverty. Cooper [1968] sums up the frustrations encountered in
poverty field work when he noted:

> Meeting, seeing, and listening to the low income people suggest
> that they frequently make decisions affecting their economic
> behavior on the basis of a nonlogical attempt to maximize their
> satisfaction . . . The poorest are frightened by their neighbors,
> public welfare workers, and the world in general. Along with this

fear they appear socially unrelated to the world and income opportunities. [P.130]

Herein lies a crucial issue. Is a subculture that possesses the characteristics just described an irrational system? What relationship, if any, does it
have with economic adversity? It is the hypothesis of this study that folk culture is not irrational, that it can be understood, and that it is functional when
viewed from the perspective of persons experiencing long-run economic adversity.

Neoclassical economics has traditionally held that the sociopsychological aspects of man to be assumed constants, exogenously determined. But
persistent economic adversity affects the sociopsychological parameters of
human nature itself. This relationship, which traditional economic analysis
misses, is central to an understanding of the noneconomic dimensions of poverty. Behavioral patterns and decision-making of the poverty-stricken simply do
not conform to the behavioral and environmental assumptions implicit in economic analysis. Contrary to the sociopsychological environment normally
assumed, decision-making in extreme rural poverty occurs under conditions of:
(1) social disintegration with regard to community, (2) low standards of living
and poor expectations with regard to the future, and (3) the shrinkage of time
horizons to zero.

Why should it be surprising if people who believe they have no
future emphasize present enjoyment? Irrationality exists here indeed—but
it is the irrationality of trying to "explain" the behavior of the poor by economic models which assume a sociopsychological and economic environment unrelated to that experienced by the poor. The task, then, is to begin with the actual conditions set out above and to develop a model in which folk culture is
rationally explicable.

Extreme care must be taken, however, in attempting alternative
model-building. Many who study poverty fail to recognize the influence of their
own values in analyzing the subject.[5] Rationality is implicitly defined in terms
of "conventional middle-class or stable working-class norms," and "any possibility of finding another kind of social organization or cultural patterning . . . is
confounded from the outset" [Valentine 1968, p. 22]. As a result, it is a small
step to a culture of poverty model in which the distinctive traits of the poor
are enumerated and emphasized in such a way that the poor are classified as a
distinct subculture. Such a model with wide acceptance in academia and govern-

5. In the culture of poverty literature, C.A. Valentine's *Culture and Poverty*
[1968] is the single outstanding work upon which this section leans heavily.

ment has been labeled by Valentine as the "Self-Perpetuating Subsociety with a Defective, Unhealthy Subculture." Its general formulation is as follows:

1. Lower-class poor possess a distinct subculture, and in the stress of life covered by this subculture they do not share the dominant larger culture typified by the middle-class.
2. The main distinctiveness of the poverty subculture is that it constitutes a disorganized, pathological, or incomplete version of major aspects of middle-class culture.
3. The poverty subculture is self-generating in the double sense that socialization perpetuates both the cultural patterns of the group and consequent individual psychosocial inadequacies blocking escape from poverty.
4. The poverty subculture must therefore be eliminated, and the poor assimilated to middle-class culture or working-class patterns, before poverty itself can be done away with.
5. These changes may occur through revolution in underdeveloped societies where the poor are the majority; in the West they will be brought about by directed culture change through social work, psychiatry, and education. [Ibid., pp. 141–142]

First, as a portrayal of the poor, this frame of reference is inaccurate. Ford, in his survey of Appalachia, made no attempt to deny the existence of traditionalism, fatalism, and anxiety, but was surprised at the degree to which conventional norms existed.

> Most of the people of the region, according to the evidence of the survey data have adopted the major goals and standards typical of American society. They, like other people throughout the nation, wish to have larger incomes, greater comforts, and more prestigful status. And if it seems unlikely that they will realize these aspirations for themselves they would at least like to see them realized by their children. [Ford 1962, p. 32]

Virginia H. Young, [1970] in her study of rural blacks in Georgia, seriously challenges the Moynihan portrayal of the black family, finding far greater stability than the culture of poverty model would indicate. Similarly, Bryan and Bertrand, [1970] in their study of rural poor in the Mississippi Delta, conclude that while the poor did in fact exhibit higher rates of fatalism and lower rates of participation, there was no correlation between these factors and the poor's propensity for change.

At issue here is the failure of most studies of poverty to distinguish, as J.M. Keynes [1965] did over thirty years ago, between aspirations and expectations in decision-making.[6] The poor are not unlike the rest of society in terms of their aspirations. However, the generally negative political-economic environment in which they live leads to much lower expectations. As the present study will attempt to demonstrate, many of the deviant cultural traits associated with the poor—for example, taking one's pleasures in any available form, be it drugs, sex, or alcohol, with little regard for the future—arise from the social stress that comes from having normal aspirations and values but little expectation of realizing them.

Second, the prevailing culture of poverty model places the blame of poverty largely on the poor themselves by suggesting that the primary problem of poverty is internal to the subculture rather than external to it. There is no recognition of the fact that the poor may possess significant middle-class or working-class aspirations and values. As a result, attention is shifted away from the remedies of redistribution of income, education, political power, and "what the rest of society is doing to the poor"and directed toward a social work program designed to encourage middle-class values so the poor can escape poverty [Valentine 1968]. As Valentine states, "in this form it is little more than a middle-class rationale for blaming poverty on the poor and thus avoiding recognition of the need for radical change in our society" [Ibid., p. 144].

My intent is not to deny that internal deficiencies exist among the poor, but to determine how they are related to external causes. The point is that the distinctive traits of the poor may be no more than "situation adaptations" to a structural environment in which they live but over which they have no control.

> The alternative interpretation is that lack of work, lack of income, and the rest pose conditions to which the poor must adapt through whatever socio-cultural resources they may control. That is, these conditions are phenomena of the environment in which the lower class lives, determined not so much by behaviors and values of the poor as by the structure of the total social system. It may be suggested also that this larger structure is perpetuated primarily by the economic and political action of the non-poor. [Ibid., p. 116]

In this light Valentine formulates an alternative model of poverty which he labels "Heterogeneous Subsociety with Variable Adaptive Subculture." Its general formulation follows:

1. The lower-class possess some distinct subcultural patterns, even though they also subscribe to norms of the middle-class or the total system in some of

6. The only social scientist making this suggestion recently is Slocum [1967].

the same areas of life and are quite nondistinctive in other areas: There is variation in each of these dimensions from one ethnic group to another.

2. The distinctive patterns of the poverty subcultures, like those of the other subsocieties, include not only pathogenic traits but also healthy and positive aspects, elements of creative adaption to conditions of deprivation.

3. The structural position and subcultural patterns of the poor stem from historical and contemporary sources that vary from one ethnic or regional group to another but generally involve a multicausal combination of factors. . . .

4. Innovation serving the interests of the lower-class to an optimal degree will therefore require more or less simultaneous, mutually reinforcing changes in three areas: increases in the resources actually available to the poor; alterations of the total social structure; and changes in some subculture patterns.

5. The most likely source for these changes is one or more social movements for cultural revitalization, drawing original strength necessarily from the poor, but succeeding only if the whole society is affected directly or indirectly. . . .
[Ibid., pp. 142-143]

The primary effect of this model is to formulate poverty in terms of *relative deprivation* and to shift attention to the social structure at large and its effect or consequence on the poor. As such, two questions come immediately to mind: How does prolonged economic adversity relate to distinctive subculture traits? How might social change in society at large create economic adversity for subgroups of the larger society? The remainder of this chapter will explore the former question, while Chapters 2, 3, and 4 attempt to analyze the latter.

Sociology has for some time attempted to explain individual personality and life organization styles in terms of an interdependency relationship between the individual and society [Mills 1953]. And as a consequence, sociologists have also hypothesized for some time that social change affects the individual in southern Appalachia. For example, Schwarzweller [1970] notes that where social change is such that the old rules of the game no longer seem to produce desired responses, people become confused and bewildered, a condition which sociologists since Durkheim have classified as anomie.[7] Consequently it is not surprising that where economic adversity has resulted in community decay, community members exhibit a high degree of anomie and psychological anxiety. As Schwarzweller [1970] states the problem:

7. Merton's anomie occurs under the condition of unavailable means for gaining desired ends. New values are substituted or new means, e.g., crime, or psychological malaise occur. See Merton [1968].

Disturbances of the social system, especially of the family system, almost by definition require a concomitant adjustment in the personality of these individuals involved. Individuals who cannot adapt, or who find great difficulty in accepting these changes, learning new ways and adjusting their lives in accord with new standards of behavior, may themselves become psychologically disturbed and experience problems of frustrations, of mental health, or personality deterioration. [Pp. 60–61]

Although all social systems have social mechanisms by which such an adaptive process takes place, the interesting question concerns itself with situations in which the mechanism breaks down or works so slowly that individuals experience prolonged economic adversity. It is to this particular question that Richard Ball [1970] has addressed himself. Folk culture to Ball is a social system built over time in response to extreme adversity. While nonrational from a "normal" point of view, folk culture serves the human need of relieving anxiety and frustrations. The question then is to build a behavioral model that accounts for the characteristics of folk culture.

Here psychology may help us. Psychology has delineated two types of behavioral patterns, "motivation-instigated behavior" and "frustration-instigated behavior" [Ibid., p. 70]. Motivation-instigated behavior is "normal" or "rational" behavior associated with learning theory. Subjects who are placed in forced-choice situations with consistent patterns of reward and penalty develop goal-motivated behavior. Such behavior is characterized as "flexible," "adaptive," and "goal-oriented," with the individual learning and profiting from his experience.

On the other hand, when the subject is placed in a forced-choice situation that is insoluble, with a random reward and penalty system, an "irrational" (nonadaptive) behavioral pattern appears which cannot be accounted for by learning theory. Such frustration-instigated behavior is characterized by "fixation," "regression," "aggression," and "resignation." The distinguishing trait in this behavior is that "the consequence of the action is not a factor in the selection of behavior" [Ibid., p. 70]. A further consideration is that once adopted, the subject rigidly maintains such behavior in the face of consistent penalty. Since it has no apparent goal, such behavior appears irrational to the observer. However, the key to understanding it is that while irrational from a goal-directed point of view, it serves the *function* of temporarily reducing anxiety and frustration for subjects who regard themselves to be in insoluble situations. In this context such behavior becomes quite rational.

The test of any model is to look at its explanatory value. Ball does this with interesting results. Tenacious adherence to custom and tradition are classic examples of fixation. Fatalism and apathy fall clearly within the category of resignation. Anti-intellectualism and religious fundamentalism become understandable as acts of regression. Finally, action-seeking and acts of aggression in response to frustration are self-explanatory. The crucial fact is that frustration-instigated behavior is a "terminal response to frustration and not a means to an end" [Ibid., pp. 74–75]. As Ball succinctly puts it:

> The subculture represents to a significant degree the institutionalization of frustration-instigated behavior, the principal values, beliefs, and implementing norms, formed during a history of contemporary life. These shared understandings are transmitted across generations; the young learning to anticipate defeat and to perform the subcultural ritual which reduces its impact. The frustration-instigated behaviors . . . have become a thorough-going way of life justified by religious doctrine and sustained by social order. [Ibid., p. 76]

The implications here challenge many assumptions of the first (culture of poverty) model set forth in this chapter. The social-work program with its concern for value change on the part of the poor ignores the fact that folk culture "may be for some the only emotional refuge available," given a constant social structure [Ibid., p. 73]. *The key assertion here is that folk culture, to use Valentine's terminology, is creative adaption to deprivation.* With the breakdown of isolation through mass media and increasing contact with outsiders, the poor do, contrary to Glazer and Moynihan, possess many of the same values and aspirations of the rest of society. However, the change in opportunities available to the lower strata of our society has not been significant enough to alter other *expectations.* As long as the nonpoor refuse to consider structural change which would redistribute income, education, and political power in favor of the poor, the latter are going to be faced with "increasing frustration based on a sense of relative deprivation" [Ibid., p. 78].

CONCLUSIONS

The study of poverty is a study of inequality, and it is indeed unfortunate that modern day students of poverty have never read or have forgotten Rousseau's *Discourse on the Origins of Inequality* [1952]. In this essay Rousseau pointed to two fundamental causes of inequality. The first was "natural" and was due to differences in age, health, mental endowment, etc. The second cause, and for Rousseau the most significant, was political: poverty was the product of social institutions and the man-made systems of privileges associated with social institutions. In reviewing the literature on poverty, one is struck by the general absence of any systematic attempt to inquire into cause, or the general inference that the cause is "natural," to use Rousseau's terminology.

As we have seen, the very methodology that has gained general acceptance in poverty studies is oriented toward identifying the poor, not seeking the cause of their poverty. The standard procedure is to determine an "objective" definition of poverty, such as that offered by the Social Security Administration which identifies all persons falling under a given income level as being poor. Having identified the poor, the next step consists of identifying a distinctive set of personal characteristics associated with the various subgroups of the poor. Usually this includes considerations of race, age, education, health, family size, number of dependent children, etc. However, this entire approach has serious shortcomings. First, as we have shown, the attempt to define some objective measure of poverty not only avoids the whole question of income distribution but is a value-laden measure in its own right. Second, the innumerable studies of distinctive personal characteristics of the poor beg the question—why do some subgroups of our society possess a set of undesirable characteristics while others do not? The whole approach to date has been to treat poverty as a distinctive phenomenon to be studied in micro terms rather than as a distribution problem related to social structure in society as a whole.

Where there has been some concern for causes of poverty, a cultural deviation thesis has generally been advanced as an explanation. But as Valentine has pointed out, the culture of poverty thesis comes close to being a rationale for blaming poverty on the poor. A fundamental problem with this thesis centers around the question as to whether cultural deviance is the cause or the result of prolonged economic deprivation. As has been shown, there is strong reason for believing it is the latter. Virtually all of the culture of poverty thesis studies have failed to distinguish between *expectation* and *aspiration,* and between *behavior* and *values.* Studies presented above by Ford, Young, and Bertrand all found a level of aspirations generally similar to that of middle-class America. The difference lies with expectations, with the poor characterized as having low or negative expectations of realizing those aspirations. Given significant deviation between aspiration and expectations, the individual is confronted with a situation of stress which he relieves by a variety of behavioral responses such as aggression, resignation, and fatalism. The fundamental mistake made by the sociologist has been to observe behavioral patterns associated with negative expectations and to conclude that he was observing distinctive cultural values producing different aspirations.

In order to alleviate poverty it is necessary to determine and eliminate factors that cause poverty. To determine causes that are political it is necessary to look at the distributional consequences of social structure in society as a whole. Consequently the next chapter will trace the change that has occurred in Southern agriculture and examine the consequences for Appalachia and the Core South. After that we will assume the task of analyzing the underlying factors that brought about this structural change.

Chapter Two

Structural Change in the Rural South: 1935-1966

The South cannot be fully understood merely as a geographic area possessing certain distinctive economic characteristics. As the eye ranges over columns of figures distinguishing the South from the North, the question comes to mind— why the difference?

Part of the answer lies with the recognition that the South is not only an area but a state of mind. Out of its mental set come values, beliefs, habits of thought, and particular social relations which cause, filter, and differentiate social change. In addition to describing the Southern mind and its evolution over time, Cash makes a major contribution by exposing the popular distinction of "old South" and "new South" as myth.

The old South is usually pictured "as a sort of stage piece out of the eighteenth century, wherein gesturing gentlemen moved soft spokenly against a background of rose gardens, dueling grounds and lovely ladies in farthingales . . . wholly dominated by ideals of honor and chivalry and noblesse" [Cash 1941, p. ix] . This, according to popular mythology, was swept away by the Civil War and Reconstruction and in its place arose a new South: modern, industrial, and democratic in outlook.

There *was* an old South and there *is* a new South, but they were not of this order. By the late thirties, change had come to the South, but the break between the new and the old has been "vastly exaggerated" [Ibid., p. x] . In the long sweep of Southern history the outstanding characteristic is continuity, and the degree to which the roots of the new South lie in the old. In Cash's words:

> Proud, brave, honorable by it lights, courteous, personally generous, loyal swift to act, often too swift, but signally effective,

sometimes terrible in its actions—such was the South at its best. And such it remains today, despite the falling away in some of its virtues. Violence, intolerance, aversion and suspicion toward new ideas, an incapacity for analysis, an inclination to act from feeling rather than thought, an exaggerated individualism and a too narrow concept of social responsibility, attachment to fiction and false values, above all too great attachment to racial values and a tendency to justify cruelty and injustice in the name of these values, sentimentality and a lack of realism—these have been its character-istic vices in the past. And, despite changes for the better they remain its characteristic vices today. [Pp. 439–440]

In light of this analysis, it should not be surprising that the South spent the first decade after World War I in religious fundamentalism. Its answer to the gathering tensions of the twenties was to "withdraw into the past and revere an exaggerated simplicity of religious beliefs and dogma" [Ibid., pp. 341–350].

STRUCTURAL CHANGE

The South turned the decade into the thirties with an agriculturally dependent, mule-powered economy. This is true of the Appalachia region as well as the Core South. Of the 920,000 tractors on farms in 1930, only 16 percent were in the South [Myrdal 1944]. In general, well under 20 percent of the farming opera-tions of breaking land, disking, and harrowing were performed by tractor power (see Table 2-1). This compared to a national average of over 50 percent for the same operations [Fulmer 1950]. For all practical purposes cotton was still king in the Core South. Myrdal notes that despite all the changes, "More than half of the total acreage harvested in the South in 1929 was in farms for which 40 percent or more of gross income come from cotton" [p. 235]. Even more startling was the low level of mechanization of cotton farms in the Core South. Approximately 16 percent of land preparation and 4 percent and 6 percent, respectively, of planting and harvesting was performed by tractor power as late as 1939.

The dominant form of farm organization in the Core South was the tenant system. Owner-operated farms continued their late nineteenth cen-tury decline by decreasing from 53 percent of all farm operators in 1910 to 44 percent of all farm operators in 1930 (see Table 2-2). The number of tenants rose by approximately 550,000 during the same period, reaching 56 percent of all operators [Myrdal 1944]. The increase extended to both black and white tenants, with some 400,000 (nearly 63 percent) of the increase being white and the rest being black.

Table 2-1. Importance of Tractor Power in Performing Major Operations of Specified Enterprises by Regions[a]: 1939 and 1946

Enterprise and Operation	*Percentage of Total of Specified Operations Performed by Tractor Machines*							
	Southeast		*Delta*		*Corn Belt*		*U.S.*	
	1939	1946	1939	1946	1939	1946	1939	1946
All crops:								
Breaking land	12	38	11	35	69	92	55	82
Disking	23	53	19	48	69	92	57	85
Harrowing . . .	9	31	9	29	52	86	43	77
Small grains:								
Breaking land	13	41	26	42	71	91	71	90
Disking	24	56	36	55	70	92	70	91
Harrowing . . .	10	32	23	38	54	85	58	85
Drilling seed . .	7	36	23	38	30	70	49	79
Harvesting	32	62	35	54	71	91	69	90
Corn:								
Breaking land .	11	36	13	32	73	92	51	78
Disking	21	51	21	45	72	93	53	81
Harrowing . .	9	30	11	25	56	87	39	72
Planting	2	13	4	12	9	44	13	41
Cultivating . .	3	10	5	16	47	82	30	64
			Mid-South		*Mtn. Pacific*			
Cotton:								
Breaking land	10	38	16	42	81	94	30	60
Harrowing . .	8	29	13	37	67	89	25	54
Planting	2	13	4	16	64	81	21	43
Cultivating . .	2	11	6	18	69	87	21	45

[a]Regions are broken down as follows: Southeast = Virginia, North Carolina, Georgia, Florida, Alabama; Delta = Mississippi, Arkansas, Louisiana; Cornbelt = Ohio, Indiana, Illinois, Iowa, Missouri; Mid-South = the Delta states plus Tennessee and Missouri; Mountain Pacific = New Mexico, Arizona, California.

Source: Fulmer, 1950, p. 63.

What is most interesting about the tenancy system was its almost total dependency on cotton as compared to owner-operated farms. In 1929 approximately three-fourths of all Southern cotton farms were operated by tenants. This contrasts with owner operators of which only one-third had farms where cotton accounted for 40 percent or more of gross receipts. In short, approximately "three-fourths of all croppers and two-thirds of all tenants worked on cotton farms" [Ibid., p. 233].

The position of the black was even more precarious. The black population has always been concentrated in the Core South. Not only was it concentrated in cotton farming, but its socioeconomic status was primarily that of tenant and day laborer. Of the 880,000 black operators in 1930 only 186,000

Table 2-2. Number and Percentage Distribution of Farms, by Color and Tenure of Operator, for the South: 1910 to 1964

Color and Tenure of Operator					Number and Percent of Farms					
	1910 (000)	1910 (%)[a]	1920 (000)	1920 (%)	1925 (000)	1925 (%)	1930 (000)	1930 (%)	1935 (000)	1935 (%)
All farm operators	3,098	100.0	3,207	100.0	4,141	100.0	3,224	100.0	3,422	100.0
Full owners	1,329	42.9	1,406	43.8	1,333	42.6	1,191	36.9	1,340	39.2
Part owners	215	6.9	191	6.0	186	5.9	225	7.0	235	6.9
Managers	16	0.5	18	0.6	11	0.3	17	0.5	16	0.5
Tenants	1,537	49.6	1,591	49.6	1,601	51.1	1,791	55.5	1,831	53.5
White:										
Total	2,207	100.0	2,284	100.0	2,300	100.0	2,342	100.0	2,606	100.0
Full owners	1,154	52.3	1,227	53.7	1,174	51.0	1,050	44.8	1,190	45.7
Part owners	172	7.8	152	6.7	151	6.6	183	7.8	199	7.6
Managers	15	0.7	17	0.7	10	0.4	17	0.7	15	0.6
Tenants	866	39.2	888	38.9	965	42.0	1,091	46.6	1,202	46.1
Nonwhite:										
Total	890	100.0	923	100.0	831	100.0	882	100.0	816	100.0
Full owners	175	19.7	179	19.3	160	19.2	140	15.9	150	18.4
Part owners	43	4.9	39	4.2	35	4.2	42[b]	4.7	36[b]	4.4
Managers	1	0.1	2	0.2	[b]	0.1	[b]	0.1	[b]	[c]
Tenants	670	75.3	704	76.2	636	76.5	699	79.3	629	77.1

[a]Percentages for white and nonwhite compare only within own category. They do not reveal that in 1910 nonwhites we[re]
29 percent of all farm operators and in 1964 they were only 13 percent of all farm operators.
[b]Less than 1,000.
[c]Less than .05 percent
Source: Adapted from U.S. Bureau of the Census, 1964, p. 765.

were owner operators in some form [U.S. Bureau of the Census 1964] . The economic state of affairs in the Core South can best be summarized in the words of Myrdal: "In the main, cotton is cultivated by means of a primitive labor consuming agriculture technique which has not changed much since slavery" [1944, p. 233] .

Appalachia presents a different picture. In addition to having a relatively small black population, its agriculture has been characterized by small, subsistence family farms. In 1930 the average farm size was 86 acres [U.S. Department of Agriculture 1935] . However, over 40 percent of all farms were under 50 acres in size. More interesting is the dominance of subsistence farming— 40 percent of all farms. When consideration is given to the fact that "abnormal" farms were primarily subsistence (the only difference being that the operator worked 150 days a year off the farm), the estimate of self-sufficient farming rises to approximately 59 percent of all farms in the region [Ibid.] .

The only similarity between the regions is the general absence of mechanization. As of the 1930 Agriculture Census, only 3 percent of all farms

1940 (000)	1940 (%)	1945 (000)	1945 (%)	1950 (000)	1950 (%)	1959 (000)	1959 (%)	1964 (000)	1964 (%)
3,007	100.0	2,881	100.0	2,652	100.0	1,645	100.0	1,373	100.0
1,328	44.2	1,509	52.4	1,411	53.2	947	57.5	809	58.9
217	7.2	194	6.7	326	12.3	323	19.6	304	22.1
14	0.5	13	0.5	10	0.4	9	0.6	7	0.5
1,449	48.2	1,165	40.4	905	34.1	366	22.3	254	18.5
2,327	100.0	2,216	100.0	2,093	100.0	1,379	100.0	1,188	100.0
1,186	51.0	1,348	60.8	1,270	60.7	857	62.1	738	62.1
185	8.0	165	7.5	274	13.1	285	20.7	272	22.9
13	0.6	13	0.6	10	0.5	9	0.6	7	0.6
943	40.5	690	31.1	540	25.8	228	16.5	171	14.4
680	100.0	665	100.0	559	100.0	266	100.0	185	100.0
142	20.9	161	24.2	141	25.3	90	33.8	71	38.4
31[b]	4.6	28[b]	4.2	52[b]	9.3	38[b]	14.1	31[b]	16.9
[b]	0.1	[b]	0.1	[b]	[c]	[b]	0.1	[b]	0.1
507	74.5	476	71.5	366	65.4	138	52.0	82	44.6

reported tractors and 6 percent reported trucks. Put differently, there were 540,548 horses and mules over the age of two and three years. In 1930 there were on the average 72 horses and mules and 1.5 tractors per each thousand acres harvested [Ibid.]. Interestingly, one-third of the subsistence farms reported neither horses, mules, nor tractors.

In contrast to the Core South, mining and manufacturing provided one-fifth of the employment in the region in 1930 [Ibid.]. It is significant to note that the bulk of employment in these categories came from coal mining and textile manufacturing. As will be shown later, technological change and changing aggregate demand in these industries would tremendously complicate regional adjustment to the agricultural transition that the region would experience in the fifties.

In summary, it is possible to characterize the South as a region in which mechanization had not yet played a major role by the thirties. In social terms, maximization of profits was partially subordinated to considerations of life style and maintenance of existing social structure. The Core South was for all practical purposes a monoculture organized around a labor-intensive tenancy system using large quantities of unskilled labor. Appalachia, on the other hand, was organized around subsistence farming, supplemented by coal mining and textile manufacturing, all of which relied primarily on unskilled labor. Into this social system was injected an accelerating mechanization that was to have severe consequences for the nation as a whole.

THE AGRARIAN REVOLUTION IN THE SOUTH

The gap between national and Southern rates of mechanization started to narrow slightly during the decade of the thirties, particularly in the Core South. Myrdal [1944] notes that the "cotton South" increased the number of tractors on farms by approximately 86 percent during the decade as compared to 70 percent for the nation as a whole. More important is the accelerated rate of change that began after 1939. Between 1940 and 1945, tractors on farms increased by 136 percent in the Eastern cotton states and by 100 percent in the Delta region of the South [Fulmer 1950]. The impact of the tractor can best be seen when the farming operation is broken down into land preparation, planting, and cultivation (see Table 2-1). Between 1939 and 1946 tractor power in the performance of these operations had tripled even though there was still a significant lag between the South and the nation as a whole. Note particularly the lag in planting and cultivation of cotton, with less than 20 percent of these operations being mechanized by 1946. The real hint of what was in store for the Core South can best be seen in Table 2-3 and in the estimate that tractor drawn plows and mowers increased by over 250 percent between 1945 and 1948 [Ibid.].

Still, by the early 1940s mechanization had occurred primarily in land preparation, while harvest and chopping and weeding tasks remained hand operations. In 1944, it is estimated that only 100,000 bales of cotton were mechanically picked [Ibid.]. However, modern technology was beginning to overcome technical difficulties in these operations. In 1943 International Harvester's model picker was operational in the Delta region. The recently introduced flame cultivator was being modified to handle the tasks of chopping and hoeing cotton [Ibid.].

The consequences of farm mechanization were easily foreseen. Fulmer, using E.L. Langford's *Cotton Production in War and Peace,* gives an early estimate of the consequence of mechanization the Core South. In the Delta region, going from mule-powered preparation and hand harvesting to a completely mechanized planting, cultivating, and harvesting operation would reduce labor from 160 man hours per bale to 28 man hours per bale. Total mechanization would make possible a labor reduction of 82 percent or 116

Table 2-3.   Trends in Number of Specified Kinds of Farm Machinery in the South: 1942 to 1948

Region and Type of Equipment	No. on Farm (000)			Percent Increase		
	Jan. 1, 1942	Jan. 1, 1945	May 1, 1948	Jan. 1, 1942 to Jan. 1, 1945	Jan. 1, 1945 to May 1, 1948	Jan. 1, 1942 to May 1, 1948
Southeast[a]						
1. Tractor-drawn:						
a. Moldboard plows	63.7	77.4	288.0	21.5	272.1	352.1
b. Disk harrows	114.6	128.4	c	12.0	c	c
c. Disk plows	48.0	54.6	c	13.8	c	c
d. Disk plows—on way	18.0	22.6	c	25.6	c	c
e. Row-crop planters	12.6	20.7	c	64.3	c	c
f. Grain drills	13.6	13.7	c	0.7	c	c
g. Row-crop cultivators	46.3	76.7	c	65.7	c	c
h. Mowers	24.2	29.8	105.0	23.1	252.3	333.9
i. Windrow pickup balers	3.5	5.7	c	62.9	c	c
j. Combines	18.4	31.8	c	72.8	c	c
2. Binders[b]	99.2	90.6	c	-8.7	c	c
3. Milking machines	4.7	8.4	c	78.7	c	c

[a] Includes Virginia, West Virginia, North Carolina, South Carolina, Georgia, Florida, Kentucky, Tennessee, Alabama, Mississippi, Arkansas, and Louisiana.

[b] Of which 19 and 48 percentages in the Southeast, and Oklahoma and Texas, respectively, were drawn by tractor power.

[c] Data is not available.

Source: Fulmer, 1950, p. 68.

man hours per acre [Ibid.] . The drastic labor-saving consequences of mechanization were spelled out before the House of Representatives by the Committee on Industrialization in the South in 1947. Fulmer's analysis of the Committee's estimate deserves quotation in full.

> The tractor population in the 13 States of the Cotton South was taken as 465,000 in 1945 (estimate of the U.S. Dept. of Agri.) on the basis of the 1930–40 annual rate of growth, 6 2/3 percent, the tractor population was projected to 1,691,000 in 1965. The figure of 465,000 in 1945 allows for an increase of 210,000 between 1940 and 1945. The projected increase is 1,226,000 between 1945 and 1965. Probably by 1965 there would be no more than 2 million bonafide commercial farms averaging 50 acres each in the South and about 75 percent of 1.5 million of them would be using tractors and other mechanization. On the basis of our tractor projection to 1.7 in 1965, this would mean that there would be a trifle more than one tractor per farm by 1965. On the basis of a net farm labor displacement of 1.303 men per tractor, the Committee estimated the net cumulative displacement in the South because of prospective tractor increase at 1,598,266 farm laborers by 1965. It estimated the net displacement from the cotton-picker and flame cultivator at 518,210 workers by 1965. . . . The total displacement in the twenty-year period, given in round numbers, is 2,116,500 workers, but because of the expected population growth in the South, the actual number of farm workers would decline only from 4,897,000 in 1945 to 3,714,000 by 1965, a total reduction of 1,183,000 below the 1945 number. Even this latter figure looms large, when the number of persons in the workers' families is considered. Although we may hesitate to accept these estimates because they are too high, it is obvious that the South is in for considerable mechanization, which is overdue, and that this cannot occur without displacement of labor. Both are necessary in the interest of efficiency and higher farm income. [P.70[1]]

Higher farm incomes for whom? What was to be the fate of the 1,183,000 displaced farm workers and their dependents? Were the impending changes to take place in the interest of efficiency or in the order of special interest?

What, in fact, happened? The two full-time equivalent series for agriculture (family workers and hired farm workers) indicate a job loss of 2,291,000 for Southern agriculture between 1950 and 1969 [Marshall 1972] . Further, in terms of scale, by the 1960s a farmer in the Southeast needed *at least* 100 acres and capital of $20,000 to earn $5,000 [Ibid.] .

---

1. As cited from the U.S., House, *Hearings Before Special Subcommittee on Cotton of the Committee of Agriculture,* 80th Cong., 7 and 8 July, 1947, p. 554.

With the advantage of hindsight it is possible to see why the Committee underestimated, rather than overestimated, the agrarian revolution coming to the South. First, the Committee simply did not foresee the tremendous changes in productive capacity that would occur in the postwar years. Farm output in the twenty-five year period from 1935-1960 increased by more than in the previous sixty years. Three-fourths of the increase came from productivity increases and one-fourth from additional resources [U.S. Department of Agriculture 1966]. In this period labor inputs were cut in half and capital inputs approximately tripled [Ibid.[2]]. Even these figures fail to indicate the escalating rate of change. Of all the increase in farm productivity in the 144-year period from 1820 to 1964, over half came in the fourteen years from 1950 to 1964 [U.S. Bureau of the Census 1964].

A second major consideration ignored in the Committee's estimate was the change in crop structure which would occur with mechanization. Given increased capitalization, greater efficiency could be effected by substituting a capital intensive crop structure (soybeans, rice) for the traditional labor intensive (cotton, corn) crop structure.[3] What is at issue here is that mechanization in the Core South did not fully adapt to the intensive farming style that was characteristic of the South. Fulmer [1950] cites Green's 1947 study of the Piedmont region of North Carolina which concluded that even after allowing for custom work, "about 32 percent of the tractors were not used to capacity or anything near capacity" [p. 70]. Nowhere does the substitution process show more clearly than in Fulmer's study of the relation between the increase in farm tractors and the increase in noncotton farms. In the period from 1920 to 1945 the introduction of one additional tractor was associated with an increase of 2.5 noncotton farms in the eastern cotton states and 1.3 noncotton farms in the Delta region. While Fulmer qualifies this ratio as not fully accounting for causation, the association is strong.

A third major change brought by mechanization and ignored by the Committee was the change in economies of scale of farming. As has been previously remarked, the South had long been characterized by increasing dependency on tenant farms. The 1940 Agriculture Census brought a startling revelation— total number of tenants were declining and ownership was on the rise. Though total number of tenants did not start to decline until after 1935, the decrease in

2. Based on the research of Christenson, Hendrix, and Stevens in U.S. Department of Agriculture, Economic Research Service, Agriculture Economic Research Bulletin, *How the U.S. Improved Its Agriculture*, No. 76 [Washington, D.C.: U.S. Government Printing Office, 1964], pp. 4-5.

3. For example, between 1950-1955, while corn acreage was being reduced by over half, soybean acreage increased over threefold and rice acreage increased sevenfold.

sharecroppers began around 1931 (see Table 2-2). Between 1930 and 1945 the decline in sharecroppers was 56 percent for white and 32 percent for black croppers [Ibid.]. Farm ownership, on the other hand, rose from 44 percent in 1930 to 59.6 percent of all farm operators in 1945.

Consistent with the decline in tenants was a change in farm size. Contrary to the North, farm size had been declining since the Civil War, reaching a low of 103 acres in 1925 and holding fairly constant through 1935. But the 1940 Agriculture Census revealed 1935 as a turning point, with the average farm size showing a significant increase (see Table 2-4).

As a result, by 1964 there were, according to the Census, 819,848 commercial farms averaging 252 acres in the South compared to the Committee's estimate of two million averaging 50 acres each. Even more revealing is the way in which this increase in size came about. Given the fact that between 1950 and 1964 the number of farms decreased by 2,228,000, while land acreage in farms remained fairly constant, the increase in farm size could come about only through combining small farms into farms of larger size. In Table 2-5 this process of concentration of size can be seen.[4] In essence a dual economy existed in agriculture. The small-scale operations of $10,000 or less were being forced out, and the large operations of $10,000 or more were expanding. When it is remembered that the first two classes in Table 2-5 were concentrated in the South, the drastic restructuring of Southern agriculture becomes obvious.

In other words, the way to increase the scale of operation consistent with the new technology was to reduce the number of tenants on the land and/or to buy up the surrounding smaller operations.

What point is more important—and almost ignored by commentators including Fulmer—is that the massive change brought by mechanization also brought critical social consequences. As Myrdal [1944] so clearly saw, the changes were not ameliorative. "The Negro and white sharecropping class as well as the Negro cash-and-share tenants are in the process of being forced out" [p. 54]. When looking at current data one wonders if Myrdal realized the force of that prediction. In 1940, which was the last Agriculture Census that Myrdal had available to him, there were approximately 1,450,000 tenants in the South or about 48 percent of all farm operators. In 1964 there were only 253,000 tenants in the South or about 18.5 percent of all farm operators.

The effect of this change has been particularly severe for black tenants. While both white and black tenants were being displaced, there were

4. Because of the changing definition of farming in the Agriculture Census since 1940, it is not possible to compare farms by type. The only comparison possible for the period of 1950–1964 is by value.

Table 2-4. Average Farm Size in the North and South: 1860-1964

Year	South	North
1860	335	126
1870	214	117
1880	153	114
1890	139	123
1900	138	133
1910	114	143
1920	109	156
1925	103	151
1930	106	166
1935	109	156
1940	123	168
1945	131	180
1950	148	194
1954	166	212
1959	217	245
1964	252	280

Source: U.S. Bureau of Census, 1964, p. 250.

Table 2-5. Change in Number of Farms in Terms of Value of Gross Sales: 1950-1964

Farm Class	Change
$2,500-4,999	-439,000
$5,000-9,999	-217,000
$10,000 or more	383,000

Source: U.S. Bureau of Census, 1964, p. 977

few opportunities for black ownership. Between 1935 and 1964 full ownership by blacks declined from 150,000 to 70,800 (see Table 2-2). Nor was it surprising that blacks did not find employment as operators of the new equipment. It is at this point that economic change is "filtered" by the social system. "To operate an expensive machine is to have a position of responsibility, which, even in the rural South, must draw white man's pay" [Ibid., p. 260]. An operator must have "intelligence" and "appreciation," attributes the South has never conceded to blacks. The immediate consequence for blacks was that mechanization crowded them into the marginal position of day laborers—a position that would eventually be eliminated by the mechanization of harvesting and cultivation.

To justify this in the name of efficiency is to ignore the fact that the uncontrolled market activity had little to do with the process. To begin with, new farm technology is not generated internally in the agricultural sector. Since the turn of this century, new farm technology has primarily been produced by a publicly financed system of agricultural colleges and experimental stations. Second, it is necessary to distinguish between at least two different aspects of new farm technology—discovery and adoption. Discovery is primarily a research process by which additions are made to an existing stock of knowledge. Actual adoption of new technology into the production process by individual farmers requires that they have knowledge of the new process and the means for its implementation. Prior to the thirties, public funding of farm technology had largely been confined to discovery of new technology which was communicated to farmers through a county extension system. However, declining farm income and credit constraints in the twenties and early thirties limited the ability of Southern agriculture in the implementation of its new technology. As I will show in Chapter 3, the evolution of the price support system initiated in the thirties has provided the larger farmer with the means of implementation. In a word, it was direct government intervention into the market that played the major role.

Fulmer, writing before the fifties, cannot be expected to foresee the farm lobby transforming the agriculture program into one of the great boondoggles of this century. But one would expect the role of government to have been analyzed in the thirties and forties. Myrdal, among others, clearly saw that the Agricultural Adjustment program was politically biased, and Hardin's devastating critique of the farm lobby in the early forties established the case beyond doubt [Myrdal 1944].[5]

The ramifications of technological change and its social consequences have been highlighted by Richard Day. Using a recursive programming model, he estimates the effect of technology on the derived demand for farm labor. Beginning with the 1930s, Day [1967] applies his model to the Mississippi Delta and identifies four representative technologies:

Stage   I: Sharecropping unit.
            Mule-powered cultivation, hand-picking of corn and cotton.
Stage II: Partial mechanization of preharvest operation.
            Tractor powered land preparation and mule-powered cultivation, hand-picking of corn, cotton, with introduction of small-scale combines and hay balers.
Stage III: Complete mechanization of preharvest operation.
            Harvest still a labor-intensive operation.
Stage IV: Complete mechanization of total operation.
            Elimination of harvest demand for labor with only a very small amount of summer weeding remaining.

5. Also see Hardin [1946, pp. 635–668].

The consequence of these four representative technologies over time was to set in motion economic and social forces culminating in what Day calls the "two stage push" off the farm [1967, p. 437]. First, as shown in Table 2-6, the process of mechanization and the consequent substitution of a capital intensive process for a labor intensive process not only resulted in a substitution of capital for labor but also changed the structure of the labor market by raising the demand for skilled and decreasing the demand for unskilled labor. The effect of technology here was not only to decrease the total number of jobs available but also to raise the demand for skilled relative to unskilled workers.

Second, with a capital-intensive process already developed, there occurred a change in crop production patterns. Capital-intensive crops (soybean, rice) were introduced in place of the traditional labor-intensive crops (cotton, corn), thereby creating a second labor-substituting process. The effect of these changes can be seen by tracing their effect through the four stages set forth earlier. Stages II and III eliminated all preharvest hand labor except for some summer weeding, although at the peak time of harvest, demand for labor remained. The consequence of eliminating one of the seasonal peaks for labor was to render the maintenance of the sharecropper uneconomical [Ibid.]. In its stead a small resident labor force was preferred, with seasonal needs met by hired

Table 2-6. Average Labor Input per Unit of Output Estimated by the Model

Year	Cotton (hrs/cwt)			Corn (hrs/bu)		
	Unskilled labor	Skilled labor	Total	Unskilled labor	Skilled labor	Total
1940	33.5	.32	33.82	1.2	.20	1.40
1941	33.0	.36	33.36	1.1	.20	1.30
1942	32.5	.40	32.90	1.4	.17	1.57
1943	32.5	.44	32.94	1.2	.20	1.40
1944	32.4	.51	33.21	1.2	.20	1.30
1945	32.6	.51	33.21	1.1	.21	1.31
1946	23.5	1.07	24.57	1.0	.21	1.21
1947	22.4	1.13	23.53	1.0	.21	1.21
1948	23.3	1.16	22.46	1.0	.21	1.21
1949	19.4	1.30	20.70	1.0	.23	1.23
1950	11.5	1.45	12.95	1.0	.34	1.34
1951	8.4	1.64	10.04	1.0	.37	1.37
1952	3.0	1.82	4.82	1.3	.10	1.40
1953	5.2	1.91	7.11	.8	.30	1.10
1954	4.5	1.89	6.39	.7	.33	1.03
1955	4.0	2.02	6.02	.7	.10	.80
1956	3.1	2.29	5.39	.4	.23	.63
1957	2.4	2.50	4.90	.3	.20	.50

Source: Day, 1967, p. 438.

labor. The consequence, as can be seen in Tables 2-7, and 2-8, was the rise of rural nonfarm population and the drop in rural farm population. While the initial effect has been to dislocate labor, it did not wholly sever labor's relationship with the agriculture sector. This second step, almost complete severance, occurred in Stage IV with the complete mechanization of the fall harvest operation. Labor, because it was no longer needed in significant amounts for the harvest operation, was forced out of agriculture and into other ways of life [Ibid.]. This occurrence is observable in the population movements shown in Tables 2-7 and 2-8.

Although Appalachia had been in serious economic trouble since the early twenties, the region exhibited greater stability from the mid-thirties to the early fifties. Primarily due to the lack of land suitable for mechanized farming, the rate of mechanization was low in this period; as a consequence, 70 percent of the commercial farms in Appalachia had sales of less than $2,500 in 1950 [Coltrane and Blaum 1965].[6] In addition to the fact that there was less pressure on labor to leave agriculture, the growth of nonagricultural employment, particularly coal mining, tended to absorb those making the shift. This did not mean that socioeconomic conditions were improving in the mountains, but rather that changing economic conditions were such that the region marked time until 1950. Thereafter, the inability of the small commercial farm to compete with large subsidized operations during the fifties, as well as automation of coal mining, produced one of the most disastrous decades in Appalachia's long history.

Between 1950 and 1959 the number of commercial farms in the region declined by 38.8 percent. More revealing than the regional average is the change broken down by farm class (see Table 2-9).

The decline in farms was confined entirely to the last class. Here the rate of elimination was in excess of 50 percent. In 1950 only 4 percent of all farms had sales that averaged $10,000 or more. By 1959 this class had risen to 17 percent of all farms, and the "$2,500 operations" had declined from 70 percent of total farms to approximately 34.8 percent of total farms. Unable to compete with the larger farms, the marginal operators were forced out; as a result, jobs declined in agriculture by 335,000 during the decade [Ibid.].

Simultaneous with this structural change in agriculture came a radical transformation of the coal fields. Having failed to defeat the United Mine Workers' challenge to their power over the coal fields, the coal companies opted for a new strategy in the postwar era. In essence this strategy was to liquidate

6. The data on Applachia is based on the 1962 survey of that region. This geographic definition of Appalachia differs from the one offered at the outset of this study. The data is presented here because a rough attempt at disaggregation suggests that the only effect of this redefinition would be to present an even more bleak picture for the Southern mountain region.

Table 2-7. Decile Population Data

Population	Delta (000)			Mississippi (000)			U.S.A. (mil)		
	1940	*1950*	*1960*	*1940*	*1950*	*1960*	*1940*	*1950*	*1960*
Rural farm	316	227	119	1400	1097	543	30	23	13
Rural nonfarm	51	66	128	351	475	814	27	31	40
Urban	63	87	121	433	607	821	74	96	125

Source: Day, 1967, p. 442.

Table 2-8. Percentage Change in Population

Population	Delta			Mississippi			U.S.A.		
	1940–1950	*1950–1960*	*1940–1960*	*1940–1950*	*1950–1960*	*1940–1960*	*1940–1950*	*1950–1960*	*1940–1960*
Rural farm	-19	-54	-62	-22	-50	-62	-23	-43	-56
Rural nonfarm	30	93	151	35	71	132	14	29	48
Urban	38	39	90	40	35	89	30	30	67

Source: Day, 1967, p. 443.

Table 2-9. Change in Number of Farms by Farm Class: 1950-1959

Farm Class	Change in Number of Farms by Value of Sales, 1950-59
10,000 or more	19,300
9,999 – 5,000	9,600
4,999 – 2,500	2,800
2,500 or less	–148,500

Source: Coltrane and Blaum, 1965, pp. 44–45.

all interests in real estate, trade, and services brought about by the operation of company towns and to concentrate primarily on achieving efficient automated coal production, ignoring any social consequences. As a result of the decreasing demand for coal and the automation of production, employment in mining declined by 265,000 from 1950 to 1960 [Ibid.].

In the face of a regional decline in employment of approximately 600,000 in mining and in agriculture, the question arises as to other employment opportunities in the region. A simple approach to this question is to net the changes in manufacturing, trade, services, and construction and then to compare the results. Such an approach would show a net increase in nonagricultural employment of 568,000, leaving a net loss of only 32,000 jobs in the region for the decade of the fifties [Ibid.]. But such an approach is highly misleading. Marginal farmers and coal miners do not become doctors, lawyers, or public administrators. Any analysis of the socioeconomic characteristics of the unemployed farmer or miner compared to the skills and attitudes associated with the new jobs being created in the nonagricultural sector makes it clear how limited the employment alternatives were for the displaced. For example, in the trade and service sector, employment rose by 341,000 jobs, but approximately half of that increase occurred in the professional category. Equally improbable was the likelihood of displaced farm workers being employed in the fields of public administration, insurance, or real estate. Thus well over half of the increase in employment was in areas in which unskilled or low-skilled agricultural workers and miners could not qualify. Dunn, using a definition of Appalachia and the Core South that approximates the ones used in this study, has analyzed the changing employment structure for the two regions from 1939 to 1958. It is his conclusion that the fast growth industries have absorbed approximately half of the agricultural decline in Appalachia and a little more than a quarter of the agricultural decline in the Core South [Dunn 1962].

CONCLUSIONS

In summary, the South between the years of 1935 and 1966 experienced an agricultural transformation that was unprecedented in its long history. The primary effect of massive capitalization and new farm technology was to displace large numbers of low-/or unskilled workers that could not be absorbed by the nonagricultural sector. In Appalachia the fifties brought the first population decline in its history. The stark consequences of this structural change for rural blacks can be seen clearly in Table 2-10 which shows the white-nonwhite differ-

Table 2-10. Summary of Changes in Socioeconomic Status of Whites and Nonwhites, by Residence, in Fourteen Southern States: 1950–1960

Measure of Socioeconomic Status	*Widened, 1950–60* Rural Urban	Nonfarm	Farm	*Narrowed, 1950–60* Rural Urban	Nonfarm	Farm
Economic:						
Unemployment rate	6	9	13	8	5	1
Percent employed in white-collar jobs	5	7	14	9	7	0
Median income of families and unrelated individuals	9	10	14	4	4	0
Education:						
Percent 15-year-olds retarded in school	0	1	2	14	12	11
Percent persons 25–29 years old with 12 or more years of school completed	2	7	13	12	6	0
Demographic:						
Average size of household	14	13	13	0	0	0
Percent children 5–9 years old in families where head is not their parent	4	9	12	9	4	1
Number of children ever born to women 35–39 years old	13	8	8	0	2	2
Housing:						
Percent dwelling units with 1.01 or more persons per room	13	14	14	1	0	0
Percent dwelling units with hot and cold piped water inside structure	0	14	14	14	0	0
Percent dwelling units in sound condition	0	2	5	14	12	9
Sum of frequencies	66	94	122	85	52	24

Source: U.S. Dept. of Agriculture, 1966, p. 122.

ences for fourteen Southern states from 1950 to 1960. With the single exception of one state in one category, the white-nonwhite differential widened for all economic categories for all states. Nor does the picture improve when education, housing, and demographic factors are taken into consideration. Further, there is current evidence suggesting that the racial income gap widened between 1960 and 1965. "All Negro farmer operators gained only $76 in income ($1,371 to $1,447) between 1960 and 1965 as compared with a gain of $1,025 for non-Negroes ($2,734 to $3,759) [Marshall 1972].

Forced out of a nineteenth century agricultural system that had persisted into the twentieth century, ill-equipped in socioeconomic terms to take part in the new industrial society, and denied the opportunity when opportunity for upward occupational shifts arose, the Southern black like his white counterpart in Appalachia was forced out of agriculture with two choices open to him: stay and starve, or migrate and hope to do better.

Chapter Three

The Politics of Agrarian Transformation

In Chapter I it was argued that rural poverty could not be understood except within the context of social change for society as a whole. Therefore, in Chapter 2 the major characteristics of the agrarian revolution experienced by the South since the mid-thirties were outlined. It is not enough to know, however, that beginning in the mid-thirties the South began a process of agrarian transformation that would revolutionize its agriculture by the mid-sixties. Nor is it sufficient when analyzing rural poverty to establish the fact that the above transformation was labor-displacing in the aggregate. To understand rural poverty fully, it is necessary to look at the basic causes of this transformation. Were they primarily initiated in response to the dictates of the market and efficiency or were they primarily in response to public intervention and the dictates of political power? This issue is fundamental to the study of rural poverty because if the causes of the agrarian transformation are caused by the market, then poverty can be explained in terms of inefficiency, and a set of policy measures would be recommended accordingly. On the other hand, if the agrarian transformation is associated with political intervention, then the explanation of poverty does not lie in the realm of market inefficiency, and quite another set of policy measures would be appropriate. It is my contention that political rather than market considerations lie behind the twentieth century transformation of Southern agriculture. In order to establish this fact it is necessary to trace the evolution of national farm policy and its impact on the agrarian sector.

By the turn of this century, American agricultural policy had changed its emphasis from land disposition to increasing agricultural productivity through publicly financed research and development. Change that began with the creation of land grant colleges in 1862 and experiment stations in 1887 culminated in the Agricultural Extension Service, established in 1914 as the implementing agency for research coming out of land grant colleges and agricultural experiment stations [Rohrer and Douglas 1969]. To augment the establishment of a network of county extension agents, the Smith-Lever Act of 1914 authorized the financing of county extension agents by federal, state, and local (including private) funds [Ibid.].

Through World War I an agricultural policy oriented toward publicly financed research seemed satisfactory. But the twenties brought a new set of problems. The legacy of the war for American agriculture was overexpansion, low prices, high interest rates, and general problems of credit. Even the literature takes on a different tone, with problems of price inelasticity of demand, and inadequate sources of farm credit dominating academic journals and newspaper accounts of farm meetings. However, with the single exception of the Farm Board established in 1929 by Hoover [Ibid.], farm policy did not undergo any fundamental transformation in the twenties. In 1930, the agricultural sector which had displayed weakness throughout the twenties was collapsing and by 1933, as Roosevelt took office, it was obvious that research and development was not the answer.

The New Deal's immediate task was to shore up the economy. Agricultural policy, like other policy, was characterized by a series of legislative measures—often not clearly defined and frequently overlapping in jurisdiction—designed to provide immediate relief. By 1938 this mass of agricultural legislation had been reorganized into two different agricultural programs. The Agriculture Adjustment Act, a series of price support measures designed to aid the normally successful farmer, and the Federal Securities Administration, a series of direct action programs designed to aid the rural poor. The combined effect of these two programs was to initiate a second phase of public involvement in agriculture. The public purse was not only assuming the responsibility for agricultural research; now it was assuming the responsibility for maintaining farm income as well. It is only by tracing the evolution of these programs and their impact on agriculture that rural poverty can be fully understood.

In observing the agrarian scene in the early forties, Myrdal [1947] noted:

> That of all the calamities that have struck the rural Negro people in the South in recent decades—soil erosion, infiltration of white tenants into the plantation areas, the ravages of the boll weevil, the southwestern shift in cotton cultivation—none had such grave consequences, or threaten to have such lasting effect, as the combination of world economic trends and federal agricultural policy initiated in the thirties. [P. 251]

We shall see, now that the results of the fifties and sixties are in; that the above statement is not confined to blacks but extends, with time lag, to white tenants and the traditional family farm as well.

THE FARM BUREAU

To trace the evolution of federal agricultural policy it is necessary to look at the impact of the farm lobby which, during the time of this study, was for all practical purposes the Farm Bureau.

The interdependency of the Farm Bureau and the U.S. Department of Agriculture has not only been documented by independent research,[1] but has been acknowledged by the Farm Bureau in Kile's [1921] officially endorsed history of the Bureau as well as in official pamphlets of the Bureau.

> The history of the development of the Farm Bureau is so interwoven with the history of the development of the extension service of the U.S. Department of Agriculture, the two institutions have so reacted on each other, that it is impossible to sketch the one without mentioning the other. [McCune 1956, p. 17]

The Bureau, born in the Chamber of Commerce in Binghamton, New York, by businessmen fearful of the militancy in the agrarian unrest [Ibid.] received a major shot in the arm by the Smith-Lever Act of 1914. The purpose of the Smith-Lever Act was to create a decentralized county agent extension system subject to local control. The county Farm Bureau was the logical farm organization to undertake the task of local finance and, thereby, local control of county agents. In 1918 the extension agents passed a resolution at their convention calling for further development of the Farm Bureau and its political activities [Rohrer and Douglas 1969].[2] Whether growth in the Farm Bureau resulted in growth of extension or whether growth in extension resulted in growth in the Farm Bureau is a moot question. According to McCune, "eventually about half of the states designated by law or agreement the county Farm Bureau as the fund raising agency for expenses of county extension agents . . . [1956, p. 16].[3]

In 1919-20 the various state organizations of the Farm Bureau were federated into a national organization concerned with national farm policy [Campbell 1962]. With the expansion of extension service and Farm Bureau

1. See McCune [1956] and Hardin [1946, pp. 635-668].
2. In 1919 Secretary of Agriculture Houston called on farmers to join or form farm bureaus in order to stop "bolshevism" [McConnell 1953, p. 48].
3. It was not until 1954 that Congress took legislative action requiring the separation of the extension service from private interest associations.

membership in the twenties, the Bureau was well established by 1930 as the major farm organization. With its membership drawn largely from middle and upper income groups in farming [McConnell 1953] and with a conservative ideology more common to the small businessman than to previous farm movements, the Farm Bureau influenced agricultural policy at two levels. First, through its lobby power in Congress the Bureau exercised a major influence on federal farm policy. Second, through its control of the county extension system, the Bureau had major control over the implementation of farm legislation as it was passed.

THE AGRICULTURE ADJUSTMENT ACT (AAA)

As was pointed out earlier, economic thinking in the twenties was dominated by considerations of price and credit, and, in many ways, the programs initiated under the New Deal reflected these ideas. The AAA can be summarized as four basic interacting programs:

1. Limitation on output.
2. Government purchase of surpluses in the market.
3. Incentives to increase soil conservation.
4. Direct subsidy to farmers taking part in the program [Myrdal 1944].

Essentially, the first three measures were aimed at reducing supply and thereby raising price, while the last was a direct subsidy designed to supplement farm income. In other words, the AAA offered a cash payment to farmers in return for acreage reduction and increased soil conservation. Average farm income was to be raised in the process by higher prices, supplemented by a direct cash subsidy payment to the farmer.

The only distributional question raised was the parity of farm income with income in the nonagricultural sector. But, as Myrdal [1944] has pointed out, parity formulated in this manner focuses on the average income for the agricultural population as a whole and ignores the problem of distribution of income *within* the farm sector. Given significant differences in economic conditions among various farm groups within agriculture, one cannot assume that needs are similar among the various farm groups or that price increases in a few basic commodities will solve the needs of all the various groups involved. The consequence for an agriculture program that ignores this problem is that there is no way it can be implemented in a socially neutral manner [Ibid.]. Consequently, in this study we are not interested in whether the AAA successfully raised *average* farm income as much as we are interested in the *distribu-*

tional impact of the AAA and its relation to the massive decline in tenancy and family farms that begain in the mid-thirties. To investigate these problems it is necessary to look at the impact of acreage reductions as well as direct AAA payment.

Acreage reduction in a landlord/tenant economic system organized around a labor-intensive production process by definition affects tenants. Acreage restriction decisions by landlords are in effect acreage restrictions imposed on tenants, and where the reductions are substantial and production is labor intensive, redundant labor is created.

The results can be seen quite simply. In 1932, the last year before the AAA, the South harvested 39 million acres of cotton. In 1933, due to the AAA, 29 million acres were harvested. By 1941, the cotton harvest was down to 22 million acres [Ibid.]. What happens to the labor that these 17 million acres previously absorbed? First, acreage restriction existed on the other basic commodities produced in the South. Second, breakthroughs in farm technology had resulted in a significantly higher level of capitalization in grains and commodities grown outside the South. Any substitution of these commodities for traditional Southern commodities would in essence be the substitution of a relatively capital-intensive production process for a labor-intensive production process .[4]

When we look at the distribution of AAA payments for taking land out of production, we see that the tenant again fared quite poorly. The data on distribution of AAA payments in the thirties is still sketchy. However, one sample of 246 Southern plantations exists (see Table 3-1) [Ibid.]. Based on this sample, average annual cash payments to tenants rose from $11 in 1934 to $27 in 1937. Owners' payments were not only higher in absolute dollar value, but they were higher as a percentage of base income. Further, it should be obvious that even if tenants had received AAA payments in as high a proportion to their base income as did owners, a fundamental problem remains. Twenty-three percent of $300 is $69. Whereas $833 is a significant sum toward providing either an adequate level of living or purchase of new farm equipment, $69 is not.

Now it is possible to see the economic squeeze that was being placed on tenants and the subsequent massive decline in their numbers. Acreage reduction by owners in the South took place largely through reduction in the tenant output, with payments for acreage reductions largely accruing to the owner. Further, it must be remembered that hired labor received nothing by way of AAA benefits. Even if landlords had taken seriously the pledge of maintaining

---

4. This long-run substitution was in fact a contributing factor in the displacement of labor out of agriculture. See Day [1967].

Table 3-1. AAA Payments on a Sample of 246 Southern Plantations: 1934-1937

Payee	Year	Average Net Cash Income	AAA Payments	AAA Payments— % of Income
Owners	1934	$2,528	$979	39
	1937	$3,590	$833	23
Tenants	1934	$ 263	$ 11	4
	1937	$ 300	$ 27	9

Source: Myrdal, 1944, p. 269.

the number of tenants, this could have been done only by reducing the amount of hired day labor. But day labor was the principal means by which tenant families supplemented their income, usually by hiring out other members of the family. The act of reducing hired labor to maintain tenants would thus have nonetheless reduced tenant family income.[5]

When we turn to the question of how farmers might increase their incomes within the framework of the AAA, a second bias against tenants becomes obvious. As it was structured, the major means of increasing income available to the individual farmer was to increase output on fewer acres planted. This could be accomplished by taking out of production the least productive land and farming the remaining acreage more intensively. But marginal productivity theory tells us that additional increments of labor to an already labor-intensive production process is likely to be subject to severely diminishing returns. The rational means of increasing productivity would therefore be to substitute capital for labor. The constraint in such a process is credit, as capital tends to be expensive. However, AAA payments for acreage reduction provided the means for circumventing the credit problem—at least for middle and upper income farmers. As formulated, the AAA was biased in favor of the larger, more prosperous farmer. By the end of the thirties we were not only subsidizing research and development in agriculture but were also providing the means for implementing new technology through AAA payments. As Myrdal [1944] noted, the Southern owner had been asked to maintain the number of tenants while being given an economic incentive to reduce their number.

> Under the circumstances there is no reason at all to be surprised about the wholesale decline in tenancy. Indeed, it would be surprising if it had not happened. [P. 285]

5. Myrdal suggests, in a different vein, that there was some attempt by owners to change the status of tenants to hired labor, thereby allowing the owner to claim all the AAA payments.

One can only conclude that the Southern landlord is not unlike his counterpart in the Third World who is reducing tenancy and mechanizing under the
impact of the Green Revolution [Feder 1969].[6] The landlord is always
willing to change the status of tenants when it is in his economic interest to
do so.

THE FEDERAL SECURITIES ADMINISTRATION

The President's Commission on Tenancy[7] in 1937 added fuel to the growing
suspicion, at least in some quarters, that the AAA was not benefiting the small
farmer and tenants. As a result, a series of what were essentially welfare programs for the rural poor were reorganized and brought together in the Department of Agriculture under the heading of The Federal Securities Administration
(FSA) [McConnell 1953].

   In the FSA were located the only set of programs designed specifically to aid the small farmer and the rural poor. The basic objective of the FSA
was to make the rural poor productive members of the agricultural sector. To
do this, the FSA felt it was necessary to eliminate three basic problems of the
poor: (1) inadequate knowledge; (2) dependency on a single crop: and (3) general unavailability of credit [Ibid.].

   From the FSA point of view, when one combined these three problems with an onerous tenancy system, the poor were virtually doomed to a
marginal existence. As a result, the FSA began to initiate a vigorous program of
reform through a multiplicity of direct-action programs. Their major emphasis
was in rural rehabilitation involving debt readjustment, tenure improvement,
and the organization of marketing and purchasing cooperatives. In addition,
they initiated other programs such as low interest, long-term loans to aid tenant
purchase of family-sized farms, a resettlement program designed to shift the
poor, where possible, to more productive areas, and a series of FSA-operated
labor camps for migratory labor.[8] Although the funding of the FSA was sub-
stantially below that of the AAA,[9] the FSA had become by 1940 "the residual
legatee of nearly every human problem that was not solved by increasing the
price of a few basic commodities" [Ibid., p. 93].

6. See also Perelman [1971, pp. 21–22].
7. Farm Bureau President O'Neal, a member of the Commission, refused
to sign the report without serious qualification.
8. In John Steinbeck's *Grapes of Wrath* (1939), the government labor camp
which aided the Joad family and which was creating hostility among the large landowners
of California was an FSA camp. As we will show later, FSA labor camps in the South led
to an all-out attack by the South on the FSA.
9. Between 1934 and 1941, the FSA spent $1.2 billion in comparison to the
$5.3 billion spent by AAA.

To implement its program, the FSA began to build its own county agency system which worked directly with FSA clients, primarily to aid each rural poor family in setting up a systematic or planned program to alleviate its current economic condition. The FSA felt, and there was similar sentiment in some quarters of the AAA, that it could not discharge its responsibilities through an extension service over which the federal government had only nominal control. Or as an FSA official remarked, "If the Extension Service had met the challenge within its own sphere of interest, the FSA might never have been created" [Ibid., p. 90].

As the nation turned the decade into the forties, two distinct agricultural policies had evolved out of the thirties: the AAA, which benefited primarily the larger normally successful farmer, and the FSA, which aimed at rural rehabilitation and transformation of the rural poor. While the AAA survived without significant modification to become the base of current agricultural policy, the FSA was formally dead by 1946. To understand the sequence of events that follow, it is necessary to turn to the role of the Farm Bureau in national farm policy.

THE FARM BUREAU AND THE NEW DEAL

The Farm Bureau's relationship to the early years of the New Deal was one of frequent consultation with the Department of Agriculture and general support for AAA policy measures. There was an aura of general harmony between the Bureau and the Democratic Party [Campbell 1962]. Underneath, however, the Bureau was nagged by the fear that the AAA might reduce its power over farm policy. This is clearly expressed in the minutes of the Farm Bureau Board of Directors meeting in June 1934:

> The organization of more than 3 million contract signers (AAA signers) constitutes either its greatest opportunity in the history of the Farm Bureau to strengthen its organization or the greatest potential threat Farm Bureau leadership and prestige. . . .
> If we fail to enlist into the Farm Bureau these contract signers, it probably will be very difficult, if not impossible, to prevent the establishment of another farm organization, out of the framework of the control committees and contract signers, particularly in the states where there are no Farm Bureaus or where our Farm Bureau organizations are small in membership. [Ibid., p. 88]

As the Bureau observed the scene, the threat to its power over farm policy could come in two ways: through the organization of the AAA signers into a rival farm organization or through the centralization of control over farm policy in the Department of Agriculture in a manner that would reduce the Farm Bureau's influence. This concern for power is crucial to understanding the subsequent action by the Farm Bureau. The position taken by the Bureau in the name of "the American farmer" seems confusing until viewed in the context of a power struggle over the control of farm policy.

The announcement in 1934 by Hearst, vice president of Farm Bureau, that "membership is power, that is all there is to it," signaled that a decision had been reached within the Farm Bureau [Ibid.]. First, the Bureau established the position that the county extension agent should be the administrative unit of the AAA; and second, it determined that a massive membership drive should be launched in 1935 with major emphasis on the South [Ibid.]. While the Bureau was clear in its support of the AAA, it remained silent on the various rural welfare programs that were initiated in the early thirties. In the reorganization that resulted in the creation of the FSA the Bureau saw the very thing it had feared— a rival organization over which it had no control. The FSA upset the Farm Bureau for a number of reasons. The Bureau had never been particularly reform-minded [Ibid.]. Consequently the Tenancy Commission Report, which Farm Bureau President O'Neal had refused to sign without qualification, and the subsequent tenure improvement program of the FSA worried the Bureau [McConnell 1953].[10] Neither did it like the independent cooperatives that the FSA was encouraging among the small farmers and the rural poor. While the Bureau's membership drive in the South had been successful, it attributed its failure in Texas to the existence of a large number of independent farm coops. Most importantly, the Bureau feared the FSA county agency system which was a direct rival to their control of the county extension service [Ibid.].

What ensued between 1936 and 1940 was a growing controversy over who controlled farm policy, culminating in Wallace's resignation by 1940 and an all-out attack on the FSA by the Farm Bureau in 1941.[11] The attack was signaled at the December convention when the following resolution was passed concerning the FSA:

1. The Agricultural Extension Service should be responsible for the home and farm management phase of the FSA.
2. The loaning activities of the FSA should be given over to an independent agency [McConnell 1953].

10. Also see Campbell [1962, pp. 156–178].
11. Southern hostility to the FSA is succinctly expressed in a quotation by a Farm Bureau leader: "We thought the Farm Securities Administration was to help tenants to become farm owners; we did not know it was to reform us" [Campbell, 1962, p. 167].

The opening for the assault was launched in the Byrd Committee, set up to review the government programs that should be eliminated to aid the war effort. After a hasty investigation of the FSA conducted by the Farm Bureau in January, O'Neal appeared before the Byrd Committee in February to make the initial attack on the FSA. While stating that some programs of the FSA should be maintained, O'Neal called for a drastic curtailment of FSA operations. Further, those programs remaining should either be implemented through the Agricultural Extension Service or through an independent agency. The basis for these Bureau recommendations were a series of "inappropriate practices" revealed by their investigation. Among other things the Farm Bureau charged the FSA with:

1. Soliciting clients to maintain FSA staff and funding.
2. Following undesirable credit practices. (These ranged from charging that the FSA was burdening the poor with excessive debt, to charging that the FSA was subsidizing the poor through loans at artifically low interest rates.)
3. Misusing appropriated funds (using funds for debt repayment instead of relief of destitution).
4. Hurting the poor through impractical collective farming projects.
5. Lobbying in Congress to maintain its appropriations [Ibid.] .

When one looks carefully at the net effect of curtailment and/or transfer of FSA programs, it becomes obvious that the result would have been the abolition of the FSA as an effective, independent organization.[12]

The Byrd Committee concluded with the recommendation that the AAA be continued because it was necessary for the war effort while the FSA be discontinued [Myrdal 1944] . The Farm Bureau then moved its attack to other legislative committees such as the House and Senate Committees on Appropriations where the same charges and recommendations were repeated. The year 1943 proved to be a fateful one for the FSA. Already in trouble from the attack of the Farm Bureau, the FSA's attempt to protect the wages of migratory labor angered the South. As a result, the National Cotton Council passed the following resolution:

> We contend that the FSA, as it now operates, with few exceptions is in direct violation of our position as stated above and that it

12. Orville Kile, the official Farm Bureau biographer, in his 1948 version *The Farm Bureau Through the Decades,* cites the Farm Bureau's bold stand against the FSA which prevented, he says, a bureaucratic agency from transforming American agriculture into a "socialist" state [p. 264] .

> threatens the foundations of American agriculture and, through
> their contention for a minimum wager per hour for cotton pick-
> ing, threaten to disrupt a fair and satisfactory system that has suc-
> cessfully operated in the Cotton Belt for over 100 years. [McCon-
> nell 1953, p. 107]

In that same year O'Neal produced the following argument for cutting off FSA
funding:

> (The) 2,000,000 smallest farmers consumed on the average about
> one-half of the production of these farms and sent only $100
> worth of products to market. This group produced only about 3
> percent of the marketed crop. They do not have the land, facilities,
> or labor to produce large quantities of food. [Ibid., p. 106]

This statement, McConnell notes, is interesting because it establishes beyond a
doubt that the Farm Bureau was not only aware of rural poverty but was "un-
willing that anything be done to relieve it" [Ibid., p. 106].

By this time the outcry against the FSA had risen to such a point
that a special committee (the Cooley Committee) was set up to investigate the
activities of the FSA. For all practical purposes the Cooley Committee became
an open forum for attacking the FSA. Under the combined attack of the South
and Midwest the FSA disintegrated [Ibid.]. Its appropriations for 1944 were
withheld, and in 1946 Congress allowed the FSA to die.

THE BUREAU OF AGRICULTURE ECONOMICS

The second line of attack by the Farm Bureau was launched against the Bureau
of Agriculture Economics (BAE). In the 1938 reorganization the BAE was
elevated to the position of an "arm of the Secretary for program formulation"
[Hardin 1946, p. 638]. It was to be a staff agency giving priority to "policy
making rather than research" [Ibid., p. 638]. The result was to divide the BAE
into two parts: (1) economic investigations and (2) livestock and crop estimates [Ibid.]. By the early forties the first part had evolved into two related
components: land use planning and socioeconomic investigation which were to
be the bases of future land use planning. This the Farm Bureau also feared as a
direct threat to its role in formulation of agricultural policy [Campbell 1962].
White its initial attack was on the FSA, the Farm Bureau had established its
position on the BAE at its convention in December 1941. The Farm Bureau
proposed a five-man

> ... nonpartisan board ... representative of the nation's agricul-

> ture . . . independent with respect to other bureaus and agen-
> cies. . . . It should cover the administration of the AAA and crop
> insurance, the Soil Conservation and Domestic Allotment Act,
> Surplus Marketing and Disposal, including the Stamp Plan, Commod-
> ity Credit Corporation, the Soil Conservation Service, and the plan-
> ning activities now in the Bureau of Agriculture Economics. [Hardin
> 1946, p. 642]

At the state level programs were to be administered by state committees

> . . . appointed by a five man Washington Board from nominees sub-
> mitted annually by State Extension Directors who previously had
> consulted with state-wide membership farm organizations. . . . [Ibid.,
> p. 643]

The Farm Bureau had, in essence, set out to destroy the planning function of
the BAE. While the Farm Bureau proposals were not accepted by Congress in
their entirety, BAE planning appropriations were cut by $500,000, and at
the end of 1942 the planning program of the BAE was allowed to die [Ibid.].
There remained the economic investigation activities of the BAE toward which
the Farm Bureau now directed its ire. Again the South was to play a major role.
In 1944 the BAE undertook a study of 71 counties, one of which was Coahome
County, Mississippi, where the issue of race was raised.[13] Angered, the South
used these county surveys as a "beachhead for a general punitive expedition
against the BAE" [Ibid., p. 652]. The indignation of the South was best expressed by Congressman Whitten of Mississippi at appropriations hearings for the
BAE.

> Do you think that would be doing the American farmer any good if
> we were by legislation, if necessary, to put your Bureau back to
> gathering agriculture statistics and take you out of the socialization
> field and the accumulation of claimed data and the printing of such
> vicious attacks on the county and its people, as is done by your
> Bureau. . . . [Ibid., p. 653]

In 1946 before the House Appropriations Committee O'Neal urged
that the conomic investigation aspects of the BAE be eliminated. He stated:

---

13. Because only a few copies of the report were ever circulated and because
Congressman Whitten refused to submit a copy to the *Congressional Record* [Hardin
1946], the contents are only partly known by word-of-mouth from FSA officials who
knew of it.

> It should be prohibited from conducting social surveys, agriculture
> planning and promotion, opinion polls (except bona fide factual
> marketing studies and surveys of consumer attitudes and prefer-
> ences with respect to consumption of agriculture commodities).
> All funds for this type of work should be eliminated. The regional
> office should be eliminated as this is a needless expense. [Ibid., p.
> 667]

The Committee cut the BAE appropriations by $483,543 below recommenda-
tion, which the House accepted, and added the following restriction to BAE
activities:

> Provided further, that no part of the funds herein appropriated or
> made available to the Bureau of Agriculture Economics shall be
> used for state and county land use planning or for the maintenance
> of regional offices or for conducting social survey. [Ibid., p. 667]

McConnell [1953] noted that there were three outstanding characteristics of the inquiry into the FSA:

1. Its progressively partisan character.
2. The absence of any searching investigation into the total operation of the
    FSA.
3. The readiness with which committees—and Congress on the whole—allowed
    themselves to be manipulated by the lobbyists of the Farm Bureau.

It is my contention that these three conclusions hold for the Bureau's attack on the BAE as well. By 1946 the FSA was dead and the BAE was
reduced to the gathering of crop and livestock data. While the AAA survived,
the only set of programs designed to aid the small and the poor were abolished.
As McConnell [1953] concluded, "Such is the resolution of the problems of
rural poverty" [P. 111].

THE POSTWAR ERA

While the first half of the decade of the forties was highly successful from the
Farm Bureau's point of view, the late forties presented the Bureau with new
battles to be fought. The reorganization of the Department of Agriculture following the war had created the Production and Marketing Administration (PMA)
as the most powerful administrative government organization in agriculture.

The PMA administered acreage allotments, marketing quotas, the loan and purchase agreement program, and agriculture conservation [Christenson 1959]. The Farm Bureau displayed the same general hostility toward the PMA that it had toward all administrative reorganizations that might be transformed into a rival farm organization or toward any centralization of power in the Department of Agriculture that would reduce Farm Bureau influence [Ibid.].

The major event, and one that at the time threatened to split the Midwest-Southern coalition in the Farm Bureau, was the proposed change in agricultural policy by Brannan. The fundamental concept of the Brannan plan was quite simple. Agricultural commodities receiving support were classified according to whether they were storable or perishable. Agricultural policy would remain largely the same for storable commodities; however, for perishables Brannan offered an innovation in policy. The farmer was to sell perishables in the market at the best price that could be had, with the difference between market price and parity price being made up by a year-end check to the farmer from the Treasury [Schultz 1949].

The plan appeared at first to have something for everyone.[14] By proposing price supports at 100 percent of some new parity, it promised high income to farmers. At the same time, the plan offered lower prices to the consumer in that their agricultural prices would be market-determined without the influence of government price support to farmers [Christenson 1959].

Initially the Brannan plan, referred to in some Farm Bureau quarters as the Patton plan, presented a problem to the Bureau. The issue of rigid versus flexible price supports had divided the membership, with the South supporting rigid price supports and the Midwest sympathetic to flexible price supports [Ibid.]. The Brannan proposal of high price support consequently divided the membership, making a united front difficult. The Bureau had to resolve this split before it could effectively oppose the Brannan plan. This was finally accomplished by a compromise resolution which called for rigid price support on cotton and for flexible price support on other basic commodities.

At first, it might seem surprising that the Farm Bureau would vent its hostility toward the Brannan plan in a manner reminiscent of its attack on the FSA. As Schultz [1949] has pointed out, the Brannan plan was not directed toward the problem of rural poverty "and like other pricing measures in this field proposes to give economic benefit principally to those farmers in agriculture who are normally fairly well up on the American income ladder" [Pp. 145–146]. Yet when we view the controversy from ideological and power consider-

14. One wag is reported to have remarked, "If the Democrats put this through they will be in for life" [Christenson 1959, p. 143].

ations, the Bureau's opposition is not surprising. First, the Bureau was not overjoyed with a man (Brannan) whose association with the Department of Agriculture had been with the FSA and whose major farm connection was with Patton, president of the Bureau's one bitter rival—the Farm Union [Christenson 1959]. Second, the Bureau did not like the plan itself. Much has been made of the fact that the Brannan plan would have made the subsidy program obvious, something farmers and the Farm Bureau did not like. Further, Brannan did not consult with the Bureau in formulating his proposal, a cardinal sin from the Farm Bureau's point of view. While these are all contributory sources of the Farm Bureau's hostility, they still do not get to the fundamental issue of power [Ibid.]. If membership is power, what claim could the Farm Bureau make as a reason for joining their organization when the current farm policy was one for which the Bureau could claim no credit? Further, why join the Farm Bureau to get a check from the Treasury? In other words, the role of the Farm Bureau would be reduced to arguing about the parity. Here we get to the real issue. Since the subsidy was made obvious, any argument over parity would no longer be an issue confined to farm politics, where the Bureau had major control. Instead, parity would very probably become an issue of general political consideration where Farm Bureau lobby power would be significantly reduced.

The end result of the controversy was a foregone conclusion. Having incurred the wrath of the Farm Bureau, the Brannan plan was defeated, and the AAA as modified by the 1945 reorganization remained.

While the Eisenhower years did not bring any substantive change in agricultural policy, the controversy of aid to the rural poor versus aid to the larger commercial farmer reappeared. By late 1955 two different agricultural problems confronted the Eisenhower Administration. The Department of Agriculture finally released a study documenting the extent of rural poverty which indicated that in 1955 there were 1.5 million farmers with incomes of $1,000 or less [Rohrer and Douglas 1969]. At the same time declining farm prices were producing unrest in the Corn Belt for the large commercial farmer.

Eisenhower's response to rural poverty was not one of direct financial assistance. Instead, the Agricultural Extension Service was expanded to offer technical assistance to low-income families. In essence, Eisenhower's program for rural poverty required the government to:

1. Counsel local groups concerning their ability to improve.
2. Provide information about employment opportunities.
3. Counsel farm families attempting new farm ventures [Ibid.].

Senator Douglas labeled the bill a "Conversation Bill" and submitted an alternative providing direct financial assistance to low-income families. Douglas's bill died by President Eisenhower's pocket-veto [Ibid.].

The economic problems of the larger commercial farmer initiated a different response from the Republican Administration. In 1956, an election year, Eisenhower was willing to give direct financial assistance to farmers by raising the level of price supports to 82½ percent of parity and by attempting production controls through the Soil Bank. Under the Soil Bank, the government, in a manner reminiscent of the thirties, offered to pay farmers to take land out of production. By 1958 rental payments rose to $800 million [Wilcox 1960], without significant reductions in output. Farmers again took their least productive land out of production and increased yield per acre on land left in production by implementing new technology.

As in the forties, government chose not to undertake financial assistance to the low-income rural families while spending billions in direct financial assistance to aid the upper-income American farmer. The world of farm politics is a strange world of double standards. While direct financial assistance to the poor is deemed to destroy initiative, corrupt morality, and encourage "socialistic" tendencies [Rohrer and Douglas 1969[15]], direct financial assistance to large commercial farmers suffers none of these objections. The end result was a continuation of existing agricultural policy in the late fifties and early sixties without substantial modification.

THE SOCIAL CONSEQUENCES OF AMERICAN FARM POLICY

The major conclusion that follows from the preceding analysis is that American agricultural policy has in reality been a massive subsidy to middle-/and upper-income farmers. Not only has agricultural policy deliberately ignored the economic circumstances of the bottom half of American farmers, but it has permitted a set of policy measures to evolve which, by encouraging increased economic concentration in agriculture, has contributed directly to the economic deprivation of the rural poor. Although action by the South and by the Farm Bureau has seriously limited government agencies in the generation of social data by which the agricultural program could be effectively evaluated, we are fortunate to have a few recent studies that throw some light on the implications just raised.

In Table 3-2 we have an estimate of the cost of the price support program from October 1933 through June 1965. Total commodity cost was $38.2 billion and, when other related costs are added in, the total cost rises to approximately $47 billion. Note that five basic commodity programs—corn and feed grains, wheat, rice, cotton, and dairy products—received approximately 90 percent of the total of all commodity expenditures.

15. See also McConnell [1953, P. 106]

Table 3-2. Government Expenditures of Price Support Program: October 17, 1933, to June 30, 1965

Item	Expenditure (in Millions of Dollars)
Corn and feed grains:	
Price support costs	4,591.9
Public Law 480	1,052.1
Direct payments	4,038.2
Total	9,682.2
Wheat:	
Price support costs	3,168.3
Public Law 480	9,517.1
International Wheat Agreement	1,464.6
Direct payments	453.4
Total	14,603.4
Rice:	
Price support costs	407.3
Public Law 480	993.0
Total	1,400.3
Tobacco:	
Price support costs	43.0
Public Law 480	306.5
Total	349.5
Cotton, upland:	
Price support costs	2,228.8
Public Law 480	1,823.8
Direct payments	548.8
Total	4,601.4
Dairy products:	
Price support costs	4,183.7
Public Law 480	308.6
Total	4,492.3
Oils and oilseeds:	
Price support costs	665.1
Public Law 480	933.9
Total	1,599.0
Potatoes:	
Price support costs	478.6
Public Law 480	1.8
Total	480.4
Wool:	
Price support costs	116.0
Direct payments	468.5
Total	584.5
All other commodities:	
Price support costs	164.3

(continued)

Table 3-2 (continued)

Item	Expenditure (in Millions of Dollars)
Public Law 480	282.7
Total	447.0
Total, all commodities	38,239.8
Other costs:	
Strategic and critical materials	1,387.3
Offshore procurement premiums	1.7
Other	3.6
Ocean transportation on sec. 416	307.2
Storage facilities	13.0
Research expenses	7.8
Accounts and notes receivable	15.9
Interest expense	3,822.9
Operating expenses	855.8
Disease eradication	218.8
Wartime consumer subsidy	2,102.3
Total	8,736.3
Total, all costs	46,976.1

Source: U.S. Congress, 1965, pp. 23, 297.

Given a price support program that has spent approximately $47 billion in twenty-two years, the next logical question concerns the distribution of the program. Here we are fortunate to have Bonnen's [1968] study of the distribution of price support benefits as of the early sixties (see Table 3-3).

While Bonnen studied the distribution of price supports with regard to eight basic commodities, I have broken out five commodities common to the South. The skewedness of distribution in favor of the upper-income farmer is obvious, with the top 20 percent of Southern farmers receiving well over half of government price support benefits. Of specific interest is the cotton program which underwent a structural change involving equalization payments. Since distribution data on cotton was available for 1961, 1963, and 1964, it was possible for Bonnen to examine the change in distribution over the period 1961-1964 [Ibid.]. In every major cotton-producing state, the Gini ratio of concentration of subsidies increased.

It is extremely interesting to look at how distribution changed over the period 1961-1964. The benefits received by the lower half of all farmers reveal no basic change. This lower group received 11 percent of cotton price support benefits before the change and 10 percent after the change. The change

Table 3-3. Distribution of Price-Support Program Benefits to Farmers, Percent of Total Benefits Received by Various Percentiles of Farmers

Item	Lower 10%	Lower 20%	Lower 33%	Lower 50%	Top 50%	Top 33%	Top 20%	Top 10%	Top 1%	Gini concentration ratio
Rice (1963)	.1	1.0	3.5	10	90	79	64	46	14.2	.625
Cotton (1963)										
Southeast	1.9	3.8	6.5	15	85	76	61	47	14	.571
Delta	1.2	2.4	5.8	10	90	81	70	58	21	.656
Tobacco (1962)	1.1	3.9	9.9	19	81	67	53	36	9	.476
Peanuts (1964)										
Va., N.C.	1.7	2.4	7.7	15	85	73	58	42	11.5	.538
Southeast	1.3	3.4	7.1	14	86	74	62	46	12.4	.568
Sugarcane (1965)										
Louisiana	.3	1.2	3.8	8.2	92	84	72	57	18	.685

Source: Adapted from Bonnen, 1968, pp. 466–501.

in distribution was in the upper half of all farmers and confined primarily to the extreme upper end of the distribution scale. The top 10 percent of all farmers increased their proportion of benefits received from 48 percent in 1961 to 53 percent in 1964. If we look at the top 1 percent we see the real change. Their proportion of price support benefits jumped from 11 percent in 1961 to 21 percent in 1964 [Ibid.] .

Bonnen concludes his study on a careful note. While the data seems to suggest that substantial proportions of the agriculture price support program are regressive in their income impact in farming, there are too many difficulties in the data to prove this conclusively. But Bonnen says,

> Nevertheless, it is fairly clear that even with allowance for wide error in our data these farm programs as designed are not highly efficient instruments for assuring some minimum level of living to the lower income groups in farming. They were designed for quite other purposes. [1968, p. 504]

Another crude way to look at the distributional aspects of total government payments is offered in Table 3–4. Here we have a listing, as of 1966, of those farmers who received from the government in excess of $25,000. The analysis and data presented in Tables 3-2 through 3-4 strongly suggest that the rise of the large commercial farmer in the United States is in large part the result of his political power rather than his market efficiency.

In addition to price supports, the government has aided farmers through a series of programs designed to provide the farmer with credit. Here

Table 3-4. Farmers Receiving Payment from the Various Agricultural Programs in Excess of $25,000: 1966

No. of Farmers	Amount of Payments Received
5	$1,000,000 or more
11	$ 500,000 to 1,000,000
258	$ 100,000 to 500,000
936	$ 50,000 to 100,000
3,939	$ 25,000 to 50,000
4,919	

Source: U.S. Congress, 1966, pp. 16, 302.

again we are fortunate to have a recent study by Herr in which some of the distributional aspects of these programs were examined. I will present here Herr's [1968] findings regarding the Farmers Home Administration, (FHA), Farm Ownership Loan Program, and Rural Housing Loan Program.

FHA

In 1966 "70–80 percent of new borrowers were either not in farming or had cash receipts of less than $10,000. Even though the majority of borrowers were on low production farms, most did not belong to a chronically low income group" [Ibid., p. 531]. The data suggests that they were either young farmers just getting started or farmers experiencing temporary financial setback.

Farm Ownership Loan Program

In 1966 a minority of the recipients were lower-income farmers. There was a significant sum going to farmers who verged on slipping into the lower-income class. Herr notes that viewed in this manner, "The program makes a contribution in alleviating farm poverty by helping farmers to acquire resources so that they will not slide into a low income class" [Ibid., p. 534].

Rural Housing Loan Program

"Less than 20 percent of the borrowers obtaining rural housing loans were estimated to be farmers with low income" [Ibid., p. 541]. The major reason why the percentage is low lies in the fact that four-fifths of all rural housing loans were made to nonfarmers.

Herr gently concluded that alleviation of poverty through specialized credit programs of the size and nature of those operated by the government in 1966 "would take a long time."

Finally, it is necessary to look at the data in terms of whether or not research and development undertaken by the government has been labor-displacing. Wallace and Hoover [1967], using cross-sectional data, introduced research and extension expenditures in their demand equation in an attempt to measure the effect of technical change on the demand for labor. As long as the product market was held constant, the effect of technical change was to increase the demand for labor. When this assumption was dropped and inelasticity of demand was assumed, they found that the effect of technical change was labor-displacing. Schuh [1968], concluded that, based upon his own studies in addition to a review of related studies, "It would appear that the flow of technology to agriculture is creating low income problems" [P. 183].

There exists one interesting study by the U.S. Department of Agriculture that related indirectly to the findings just summarized. In a study of economies of size in farming, the Department concluded that in the sixties all of the economies of scale could be achieved by modern fully mechanized one- and two-man farms [U.S. Department of Agriculture 1967]. In other words, when farm size was analyzed in terms of market efficiency, the moderate-sized farm was optimal. The clear implication is that the large commercial operator cannot be explained in terms of economies of scale. However, the study found that profits could be increased by expanding farm size beyond the most efficient size [Ibid.]. While no explanation is offered for this finding, Charles Schultze's recent study [1972] of distribution of farm subsidies suggests one. In 1969 Class I farmers (7.1 percent of all farmers) had average net incomes per annum of $33,000 of which $14, 000 could be attributed to the farm program. On the other hand, Class V and VI farms (50.8 percent of all farmers) had average net incomes of $7,900 of which $400 could be attributed to the farm program. Schultze clearly points out that the farm program "provides benefits primarily to those large farmers who produce the bulk of agricultural output" while the small farmers "are helped relatively little by these programs" [1972, p. 111]. One could hypothesize from these findings that the explanation lies in the fact that political control over government subsidy is a major variable in farm income. The large commercial operator has circumvented the dictates of the market through government subsidy.

SUMMARY AND CONCLUSIONS

The massive transformation of Southern agriculture in the last thirty years lies in the realm of political rather than market considerations. From the late thirties to the present, the middle-/and upper-income farmer has consistently been able to control the public flow of funds into agriculture. Economic theory suggests a ready explanation. If there are too many small producers of nearly equivalent size in a sector, then there is no problem with public funding since there would be widespread dissemination and no one producer could gain a disproportionate share. If, on the other hand, the sector were characterized by significant difference in farm sizes, it is no longer possible to assume general equality in the distribution of benefits. Further, once a government administration agency comes into existence, given the organization of the larger commercial farms into a national organization with significant lobbying power, it follows that there is a great probability that the public agency will be used for the interest of the larger farmer. The results are the same as those found by Raup [1967] in his study of Third World agricultural policy: "The use of public funds for research and extension then constitute the use of taxing power to create private profits" [Pp. 280–281].

Nor can it be maintained that the process just analyzed was inadvertent. In 1940 two separate agricultural policies existed, one already biased in the direction of aid to the larger commercial farmer and a second program aimed at aiding the small farmer and the rural poor. As we have seen, the farm lobby deliberately set out to destroy the latter, and Congress was willing to let it happen.

The result has been the creation of a dual agricultural economy. Currently less than 10 percent of all farmers market over half of all agricultural output, while 43.3 percent of all farms market approximately 4 percent of all agricultural output [Bonnen 1968]. Put differently, slightly over 40 percent of all farmers had net money income of less than $3,000 [Ibid.,]. At the same time, 148,000 farms, or 4.4 percent of all farms, had sales of $40,000 or more and marketed 38.4 percent of all agricultural output [Ruttan 1967]. Massive government subsidy of the larger commercial farmer has resulted in a sectorial reorganization that has displaced large quantities of low-skilled labor whose only alternative was to turn to the nonagricultural sector in hope of employment. As Minsky has observed, "economic growth is not a very promising path for the quick reduction of poverty" in such a setting.

> As long as the reservoir of rural poor is full, a great deal of progress without any substantial improvement in the lot of the poor can take place. That is, the supply curve of low wage labor in the urban sector is infinitely elastic at some markup over the going earnings of the rural poor. As long as the reservoir of rural poor is not empty, economic growth will take the form of shifting workers from being rural poor to being urban poor. [1968, p. 576]

This raises the question as to whether or not the pipeline is about empty. While many believe that the basic off-farm migration has already taken place, Ruttan offers reason for continuing concern. As of 1965 there were 1,466,000 farmers with farm sales of less than $2,500 [Ruttan 1966]. On the other hand, when production capabilities of the larger commercial farmer are considered, some startling implications come to light.

> If total production were to be concentrated on farms such as those with sales of $20,000 or more, the total U.S. farm output could be produced on 750,000 farms. If production were concentrated entirely on $40,000 or more, the total U.S. farm output could be produced on less than 400,000 farms. It seems apparent that the technological capacity already exists that could permit production of 80–90 percent of the value of total U.S. farm output on between 50,000 and 100,000 production units. [Ibid., p. 113]

Whether or not this occurs will depend on what happens to farm policy in the future. To date, however, farm policy and the public sentiment that has surrounded it represent the ultimate in hypocrisy. Government agricultural policy has been instrumental in displacing massive amounts of labor in agriculture. Instead of assuming the responsibility for the consequences of its political action, society has explained away the plight of the rural poor in terms of individual failure.

Chapter Four

Labor Market Perversity: Consequences and Implications

In Chapters 2 and 3 an attempt was made to trace the causes and consequences of structural transformation in the agricultural sector in Appalachia and in the Core South. The major impact of this agricultural transformation was a sudden release of large quantities of low-skilled labor seeking employment in the non-agricultural sector. Communities and/or regions do not have an unlimited ability to absorb low-skilled labor at certain points in time. The alternatives for that proportion of labor unable to find employment in the nonagricultural sector are reduced to two: to remain in the region at a reduced level of living or to migrate.

Migration is commonly regarded as a desirable phenomenon producing only favorable results.

> Migration does not simply redistribute poverty; it also serves to reduce poverty. By far the greatest part of migration is in response to income opportunities. This shift of the population raises income for most migrants and probably on balance has favorable effects on the income and job opportunities of those who do not migrate. [U.S. President 1968, p. 140]

The tasks of this chapter are three. First, it is necessary to trace through the consequences of migration, which in light of recent data suggest that there are serious reasons for questioning the validity of the popular generalization. Second, we will examine the structural transformation in the nonagricultural sector which has limited its ability to absorb low-skilled labor. Finally, we will examine the implications of these findings for conventional economic theory.

For all its troubled history, Appalachia's population has shown a fairly consistent upward trend. Population had increased in Appalachia at an average rate of increase of 20, percent per decade during the 1800s, declining to an average rate of increase of about 8 percent in the decade of the forties [Brown 1970]. The decade of the fifties brought about a startling change, with population declining by approximately 3 percent [Ibid.]. Brown's study of the data indicates that the decline can be accounted for in terms of two factors—by change in the average rate of natural increase and by migration [Ibid.].

Between 1950 and 1960 the average annual rate of natural increase dropped by 3 percent [Ibid.]. Interestingly enough, the change did not follow the usual demographic pattern common to underdeveloped countries of a drop in the death rate combined with a stable birth rate. Instead, Appalachia experienced a 17 percent decline in the average annual birth rate coupled with an *increase* in the average annual number of deaths of 13 percent [Ibid.]. As we will show in this chapter, this demographic experience can be explained as a partial consequence of a selective migration pattern and the "aging of society" that results.

The second major factor accounting for declining population in Appalachia was migration. Between 1950 and 1960 Appalachia experienced a net out-migration of 1,118,000 people or an annual population loss of 1.9 percent [Ibid.]. While these losses are tremendous in absolute terms, the consequences can best be seen by disaggregation in terms of the following two questions:

1. Where were the population losses concentrated within Appalachia?
2. What were the personal characteristics of migrants?

With regard to the first question three characteristics stand out in Brown's study:

1. The bulk of the population losses was experienced by the nonmetropolitan counties (1,013,842).
2. When counties were classified according to their industrial composition, agriculture and mining counties were the dominant losers.[1]
3. When counties were classified according to median income the lower-income counties lost most heavily.[2]

1. Between 1950 and 1960 manufacturing counties had losses of 11 percent, trade and service counties had losses of 17 percent, agricultural counties had losses of 30 percent, and mining counties had losses of 39 percent.
2. Counties with median family incomes of less than $2,000 had net loss migration rates of 36 percent, while counties with median incomes of $4,000 and over had net migration losses of 10 percent.

In terms of the second question, personal characteristics of migrants, the following stand out:

1. Most of the migrants were young adults (48 percent were between the ages of 15 and 29).
2. Male migrants outnumbered female migrants.
3. Migrants possess a higher number of years of schooling than those who remained [Ibid.].

It is of interest to compare these findings with those of the 1965 Manpower Report of the President (see Tables 4-1 through 4-3). Noting the highly deceptive nature of aggregative migration figures, the Report attempts to disaggregate migration by interregional movement and to determine characteristics of migrants. The findings for the South and other selected regions are as follows:

1. The migrants were both younger and better educated than the median age and education of the area they left.
2. The proportion of men in the professional and technical occupations were nearly twice as high for the out-migrant as for the resident.
3. Relatively few unskilled and semiskilled left the area or entered it [U.S. President 1965].

What are the consequences of such a migratory pattern on a region experiencing population loss? For Appalachia the consequence of migration can best be seen by looking at the subsequent population change in terms of five-year age groups for the time period 1950-1960 [Brown 1970].

Table 4-1. Net Migration Rate of Counties by Median Family Income: 1950-1960

Counties by Median Family Income	Net Migration Rate 1950-1960, Percent
6,000 and over	+12%
5,000–5,999	− 1%
4,000–4,999	− 4%
3,000–3,999	−12%
2,000–2,999	−22%
Under 2,000	−24%

Source: U.S. President, 1965, p. 151.

Table 4-2. Selected Characteristics of 1955-1960 In- and Out-Migrants and Population of Selected Areas of High and Low Unemployment: 1960

Selected Characteristics	10 Areas of High Employment			10 Areas of Low Employment		
	1960 Pop.	1955-60 Migrants		1960 Pop.	1955-60 Migrants	
		In-	Out-		In-	Out-
Total pop.:						
Median age of males 5 years and over	34.6	27.2	26.5	32.5	26.2	27.4
Median years of school completed by persons 25 years old and over	10.6	12.4	12.2	12.0	12.6	12.6
Nonwhite:						
Median age	31.6	25.1	26.7	30.1	24.7	25.6
Median school years	9.1	10.2	10.3	9.2	10.6	11.0

Source: U.S. President, 1965, p. 153.

Table 4-3. Median Years of School Completed for Males 25-64 Years Old and for 1955-1960 Male Migrants 25-29 Years Old, by Color and Region

Region	All Males 25-64	In-Migrants		Out-Migrants	
		White	Nonwhite	White	Nonwhite
South Atlantic	9.9	12.8	11.6	12.7	11.6
East South Central	8.9	12.8	12.4	12.4	10.5
West South Central	10.3	12.7	12.2	12.8	12.0

Source: U.S. President, 1965, p. 157.

1. With the single exception of those aged 10-14, every group through 40 to 44 decreased in size, with heavy losses falling in the 20 to 29 age groups. Age group 20 to 24 decreased by 25 percent; age group 25 to 29 decreased by 28 percent.
2. All age groups from 45-49 up increased in size: age group 55 to 59 increased by 20 percent; age group 60 to 64 increased by 21 percent; age group 65 and up increased by 31 percent.

It is now possible to offer a number of implications for a region experiencing a labor migration pattern such as the one depicted. First, the region should incur over time a high dependency ratio, in addition to which the ratio should shift in composition because of the "aging" of its population. It is a population shift of this kind that lies behind the change in the average annual rate of natural increase.

Second, generally accepted prescriptive statements regarding education should be questioned. It is quite common to point out that as of 1960 57.2 percent of Appalachia's population over the age of 25 had only an eighth grade education or less. Given some statement about the high returns to education, the usual policy recommendation follows that increased expenditure on education should be undertaken. Where this had been undertaken to some degree, as it has in Appalachia, students of the region are encouraged by data showing that the number of children aged 16 and 17 enrolled in school has increased from 60 to 70 percent during the decade to the fifties [Ibid.].

Before we draw conclusions from such data, however, a number of questions must be asked. Who is to benefit from the increased input in education? If education is to play a role in regional development, the county or region making the investment must benefit as well as the individual. But if the industrial structure of the county or region is not changed, what expectation does the region have so that its new graduates will remain to put their education to use within its borders? The migration pattern just outlined implies that the consequence of education will be perverse for the region in question. Increased effort in the area of education will largely be negated by out-migration of its graduates. In other words, we have an externality problem. The sending region incurs the cost of education but obtains no significant return.

Third, any community experiencing a migratory pattern such as we have described will experience severe income constraints so that the community has limited ability to take any effective action on its own.

1. There is the burden on the working population of a high dependency ratio. The regional average for Appalachia is 928 dependents per thousand workers compared to a national average of 872 per thousand. But when one disaggregates to specific subregions within Appalachia it rises as high as 1,113 per thousand.[Ibid].

2. The rising age composition of the dependents results in a significant proportion of the community population being composed of older citizens living on relatively fixed incomes. This can be expected to present the community with increased welfare needs.

3. The index of skills turns against the community in that selective process of

migration leaves the community or region with a work force whose base falls largely in the lower half of the skill range. In other words, the community is not only confronted with a relatively small work force in terms of its dependents, but given the age and skill composition implied above, local government is severely constrained in terms of its resource base (revenue, skills) in provisioning the public sector.

4. Local governments of declining rural areas are confronted with relatively high overhead in per capita terms and a limited tax base from which to operate [Lustig and Reiner 1968]. When one looks at the tax structure, the problem becomes quite apparent. Given a large number of low-income families, local governments have small medium-/and upper-income groups to tax. Any expansion of the public sector can be undertaken by increasing the tax, which by definition means increasing the tax on the middle- and upper-income classes of a community. But where this burden is regarded as excessive, these income groups either resist the tax increase or, if unsuccessful, move to a more favorable locale. Baumol [1967] has pointed out in his analysis of the urban crisis that such maximizing behavior by the middle- and upper-income classes only reduces the community tax base further, necessitating higher burdens for those who remain.

In summary, the process of adjustment described so far leads to constraints on a community's revenue base which in turn at some point forces the community into a retrenching operation. Where must the retrenching occur? In the public sector. The causal chain is outlined below:

1. Local government can either raise taxes to provide essential service, reduce service, and/or raise price.
2. Given an inability to raise taxes, service reduction and/or price change are the only alternatives. However, such action results only in further reduction in utilization of the services, necessitating another round of price change and service reduction. The end result is either abolition or extreme curtailment of services offered. Other services such as public education and health deteriorate in quality via low salaries and general inability to obtain staff and to maintain equipment [Ford and Hillery 1968].
3. The consequence of this for a community is at first a relative deterioration of infrastructure and public sector capabilities in general. But industry does not prefer to locate in communities with inadequate systems of power, water, transportation, and education, and where the work force is primarily semiskilled.

The retrenchment process thus becomes a cumulative process of stagnation and eventual decay. Unfortunately, death is lingering rather than instantaneous. And in the long process of decay the community turns out each year a new set of poorly educated, poorly socialized young who are unprepared to take part in modern industrialized society.

Johnson [1970] has recently called attention to an unpublished seminar paper presented by Easterbrook at Cambridge.[3] From a historical perspective, social change has never been a laissez-faire process. Rather, it has been a mixture of government and private enterprise, with government taking care of the major risks and private enterprise taking care of the minor ones [Ibid.]. The significance of this chain of events is that local governments caught in the circumstances we have described are not capable of assuming the major risks of turning a declining rural area around. Modern growth theory, with its concern for achieving a satisfactory rate of increase in the aggregate output of final goods and services, has generally ignored the fact that "satisfactory" growth rates may coincide with increased inequality in the distribution of income, growing regional inequality, and massive deterioration of local communities. Yet it is here that the causes of poverty lie.

LABOR MARKET PERVERSITY

Contrary to the generally accepted position that labor migration is a desirable phenomenon producing only favorable results, we have argued that under certain conditions migration can contribute to poverty rather than alleviate it. Fortunately, there are the Hathaway and Perkins [1968] studies of labor mobility and migration in rural areas which permit a more extensive documentation of the perverse nature of the labor markets there.

Using multiple regression analysis, Hathaway and Perkins analyze farm mobility[4] in terms of the following set of attributes: age, farm employment status, proximity to employment centers, index of rurality, and race (the last a variable only in the South). They conduct their analysis in terms of net relationships instead of gross terms, since the latter is deceptive because it fails to consider the consequence of the return to agriculture by a significant number of previous off-farm movers.

---

3. Easterbrook's Marshall Lecture delivered in spring 1966.
4. Mobility is defined as "moving from some form of farm employment coverage to exclusively nonfarm employment." Migration is defined as "a change in location of employment, the smallest change being from one county to another" [Hathaway and Perkins 1968, p. 185].

With regard to the characteristics of off-farm mobility their findings are as follows:

1. Probability of off-farm mobility is highest for young, multiple-job workers who live within fifty miles of the Standard Metropolitan Statistical Areas (SMSA).
2. Off-farm mobility is not higher in low income rural areas.[5]
3. No relation was found between farm earnings and off-farm mobility.
4. Off-farm mobility varies with the state of the national economy, being significantly lower in periods of recession [Ibid.].

These findings hold for all regions of the United States with the following addition for the South:

> Mobility rates of Negro farm workers, net of the influence of other mobility determinants, were significantly lower than that of other workers in all periods.[6] [Ibid., p. 190]

Looked at inversely, Hathaway and Perkins' data suggests that off-farm mobility is significantly lower for older, single-job holders who live further than fifty miles from a major employment center. When allowance is made for race, the mobility rate is again significantly lowered.

With regard to in-farm mobility, their findings [Hathaway and Perkins 1968] are as follows:

1. Between 1957 and 1963 in-farm movers averaged 90 percent of off-farm movers.
2. In-farm movers were predominately persons previously employed in agriculture who had not been able to establish themselves in nonfarm employment.
3. Compared to off-farm movers, in-farm movers could be characterized as being older, single-job holders.
4. In terms of "rurality" the in-farm mobility rate was only *slightly less* than

---

5. The data for this study comes from the 1 percent sample of Continuous Work History maintained for administrative purposes by the Social Security Administration. It is conceivable that a coverage bias could be involved in low-income rural areas.

6. They found that black mobility rates were not only significantly lower but in periods of recession the difference was "most marked." The opposite finding in other studies using unadjusted mobility data was due, they believe, to the higher proportion of farm wage workers and young persons among blacks. The explanation of their findings is increased discrimination against blacks in periods of high unemployment [Hathaway and Perkins 1968, p. 190].

the off-farm mobility rate for low-income counties, whereas in high-income counties the in-farm mobility rate was *significantly below* off-farm mobility rates.

From these facts it is possible to draw a picture of how the labor market has tended to operate between the agricultural and the nonagricultural sectors of the economy.

1. The highest probability of leaving agriculture is associated with age, multiple-job holding, and proximity to employment centers.
2. The highest probability of returning to agriculture is associated with former agricultural employees who for reasons of age and skill could not establish themselves in the nonagricultural sector.
3. Low-income counties do not have a higher off-farm mobility rate but they do have a significantly higher in-farm mobility rate.
4. Where race is a factor, mobility rates are significantly lower.

In essence, if those who leave agriculture are primarily the young, higher-skilled people living close to an urban center, if those who return to agriculture are the older and less skilled who could not establish themselves in nonagricultural employment, and if low-income counties and/or counties that are predominantly black have lower net mobility rates, then the labor market operates perversely to the interest of low-income counties. As Hathaway and Perkins conclude:

> The attributes of individuals which determine the probability of their initial movement out of agriculture also determine their chance of remaining in nonfarm employment. It indicates that the normal operation of the labor market does not serve to reduce income disparities within agriculture or between persons employed in farm and nonfarm occupations. [1968, p. 193]

The findings of Hathaway and Perkins regarding occupational mobility tend to reinforce their findings on migration. First, most off-farm movers do not migrate when they leave agriculture. Second, the characteristics of those who do migrate are similar to general labor mobility characteristics. Migrants are predominantly young, farm wage laborers from counties having relatively higher family income and are located within fifty miles of a SMSA. In-migrants were predominantly wage workers who had unsatisfactory earning experience in nonfarm employment. However, it should be noted that of the in-migrants returning to agriculture, only 63 percent were "farm employed a year later" [Ibid., pp. 201–202].

The most significant findings of Hathaway and Perkins lie in their analysis of the actual earning experience of people who have occupational and/or locational change. On the average, the lower-income workers made larger initial gains, which suggests that mobility does in fact reduce income disparity. But as they point out, averages based on short-run earnings present an inaccurate picture. Such averages ignore the fact that over 40 percent of those studied had *lower* incomes in nonfarm employment than in their last year in agriculture. Before one can say anthing about whether labor mobility reduces income disparity, it is necessary to say something about how these gains and losses in income are distributed and what their impact is on long-run earning experience. Hathaway and Perkins' findings are significant here:

> Thus, while low income farm workers receive the largest average initial gain, in the long run there was a strong positive relationship between earnings in agriculture and subsequent earnings. This suggests that those characteristics which cause an individual to be poor in farming are likely to have the same effect in nonfarm employment. . . . Farm-nonfarm occupational mobility does not seem to close the income gap between the poor and those better off. Indeed it may widen it. [1968, p. 207]

This conclusion is diametrically opposed to the one underlying government policy (and much economic thinking in general), as evidenced by the opening quotation of this chapter. Perhaps the 1965 Manpower Report says it best:

> Unfortunately, some other parts of the South with less industrial development—and the all too many depressed areas in other regions of the country—are caught in a vicious cycle of out-migration of their best educated young people, consequently difficulty in achieving economic progress, and thus more out-migration.[7] [U.S. President 1965, p. 158]

ORTHODOXY AND ITS CLASSICAL HERITAGE

It is necessary at this point to examine the implications of these findings in terms of their consequences for economic theory. Lowe [n.d.] once observed

---

7. This raises an interesting point. Why did the 1968 Economic Report of the President ignore the data in the 1965 Manpower Report?

that anyone who sees "technological unemployment" is very likely to get into a two-front war, with the Keynesian economists attacking from one side and neoclassical economists attacking from the other [p. 229]. Still, the implications of the data offered to date lead one to risk the fray. To do this it is necessary to start with a brief excursion into the works of Ricardo and Marx where the roots of technological unemployment lie.

By the time of the third edition of *Principles of Political Economy,* Ricardo [1911] was prepared to admit to the possibility of short-run unemployment associated with the introduction of machinery.

> In the case conjectured by Ricardo, a portion of the labor formerly employed in the production of goods for the consumption of the workers is in a certain year diverted to the construction of a machine, which shall enable the employer to secure in the following year the same profit with the use of a reduced labor force. During the year when the machine is under construction, the same labor force as in previous years is employed in the aggregate, and it is maintained with the aid of the circulating capital produced previously. For the following year, however, when the machine is to be put into operation, the supply of circulating capital available in the shape of goods for the maintenance of labor will have diminished in proportion to the diverting of labor to the construction of the machine. A portion of the labor previously employed will then become redundant. [Gourvitch 1966, p. 60]

In other words, a decrease in the wage fund is associated with the introduction of machinery. While it was true that in the long run new machinery may lead to higher profits and new capital formation which might absorb those workers displaced, the length of time involved in the adjustment process was unknown. As Lowe has noted, the fundamental challenge that Ricardo presented was whether or not the market had the ability to provide for automatic short-run compensation [Ibid.]

Marx [1909] placed technology dead center in his analysis, with the consequences of technology being both the change in the structure of capital and the tendency for profits to fall.[8] For Marx, the impact of technology was to change the structure of capital over time with constant capital increasing relative to variable capital. The entrepreneur, in order to protect himself from the competitive pressure on profits, is forced into investment at higher levels of technology, but the consequence of such investment is to shift the "organ-

8. There are three excellent sources in which the importance of technology for Marx has been picked up: Lowe [1954], Gourvitch [1966], and Robinson [1947, Ch. 4].

ic composition of capital" in the direction of increased constant capital. With regard to labor, "the demand for labor grows as the aggregate capital increases" but it does not "grow in proportion to that increase" [Gourvitch 1966, p. 75]. The consequence that arises for a market system has been succinctly summarized by Lowe:

> To find productive employement for the displaced, the necessary working places—plant and equipment—have to be provided. This requires a process of saving and investment which is by no means automatically assured by the existence of idle factors, or even of surplus profits on the part of technical pioneers. . . . With growing capital intensity . . . the bottleneck of capital formation can be overcome only by a steadily increasing rate of saving or more likely, by the continuous lengthening of the adjustment period. In the interval technological unemployment persists and exerts pressure on the wage level and on aggregate consumption. Such a fall in demand for mass consumption goods will in the end affect also investment unfavourably. Instead of gradual compensation we have to expect what today we would call a cumulative deflation and a cyclical downswing. [n.d., p. 235]

What had been a shortage of circulating capital for Ricardo is transformed by Marx into a shortage of fixed capital. What had been a possible short-run market imperfection was transformed into a long-run threat to the entire system.

NEOCLASSICAL ECONOMICS AND ITS CRITICS:
A BRIEF EXCURSUS

The reply to Ricardo and Marx came in the works of Clark and Marshall and the subsequent triumph of marginal productivity theory. The problem was not in a shortage of capital but in the movement of money wages. According to marginal productivity theory, "varying quantities of labor can be combined with any given quantity of fixed capital, if only real wages adjust themselves to the corresponding change in the marginal productivity of labor" [Ibid., p. 236]. Or, any amount of technologically displaced labor can be reabsorbed by the available capital stock provided that money wages fall accordingly. For all the subsequent manipulation of Hicks and Harrod, Clark's conclusion regarding technological unemployment is still the position maintained by most neoclassical economists. Essentially it is that

> The general demand for labor (is) not lessened. . . . At its introduction an economical device often forces some men to seek new

occupations, but it never reduces the general demand for labor. As progress closes one field of employment, it opens others, and it has come about that after a century and a quarter of brilliant invention and of rapid and general substitution of machinework for hard work, there is no larger proportion of the laboring population in idleness now than there was at the beginning of the period. [1968, pp. 258–259]

At issue is not that Clark's statement is invalid but rather that it misses the point in understanding technological change as a source of *poverty*. Having formulated a reply to Ricardo and Marx, one that any quick perusal of unemployment rates seems to substantiate, neoclassical economists have seldom concerned themselves with the actual adjustment path of structural change and its consequences. What has been ignored is the possibility that technological change could be a major factor in explaining poverty, even given the validity of the above aggregative statement by Clark, *due to inequitable distribution of gains and losses of economic change.* To get at this possibility, it is necessary to dig deeper into the formulation of marginal productivity theory.

Clark's conclusion holds only under a set of assumed conditions and carefully specified definitions of capital and labor. First, the assumed conditions are those normally associated with perfect competition [Clark 1899]. Second, Clark makes a distinction between *capital* which is a homogeneous fund (value) and *capital goods* which is a set of specific instruments [Ibid.].[9] The basis of this distinction lies with Clark's differentiation between the short-run and the long-run and his formulation of marginal productivity theory at both a micro and macro level. At the micro level marginal productivity is a short-run analysis determining the level of employment, while at the macro level marginal productivity is a long-run theory of wages. As will be shown later, this distinction in capital and time resulted in a confusion that has haunted marginal productivity theory.

Finally, Clark [1899] assumes labor to be homogeneous by defining labor as being some quantity of identical labor units. The merit of this assumption was to allow Clark to concern himself with a wage rate rather than with a structure of wages for various degrees of skill. In other words, at the macro level, given competitive conditions and assuming homogeneous capital and labor, one can determine the following neoclassical results:

1. The rate of return on capital is the rate of interest.

9. See also Clark [1968, pp. 28–29].

2. The wage rate varies inversely with the rate of interest.
3. The real capital-labor ratio varies directly with the wage-rate of interest ratio.
4. Distributive shares are well defined.
5. Net national product per worker, or the permanently sustainable consumption stream, varies inversely with the rate of interest [Ferguson 1969].

To be specific, given these assumptions it is possible to determine a production function where at each point under equilibrium conditions, the ratio of factor substitution is equal to the ratio of factor prices. Consequently, if relative factors change, the least cost technique changes. Accordingly, one would derive the basic theorem that as wages rise and profits fall, techniques will shift toward increased capital intensity. The result, as Dobb [1970, pp. 1–2] has noted, is to "locate a theory of distribution entirely within the circle of market relations" without introducing any sociological data and independent of institutional considerations. Note particularly the double role assigned to the price mechanism. On the one hand, it is to provide a rate of technological adaptation consistent with the growth in savings, capital accumulation, and markets for commodities, while on the other hand, it is to reallocate any displaced labor in the process of technological change.

It is a beautiful world, but the reason for the emphasis here is that J.B. Clark's "fairy tale" not only underlies modern economic theory but is still regarded by many as a useful and satisfactory approximation of reality.[10]

Yet, there are serious reasons for having reservations about the world that many neoclassical economists see. The limitations of the assumption of perfect competition were pointed out early by Wicksell, and, as noted by Kaldor [1959–60[11]], "Once capitalists act in collusion the marginal productivity theory of interest and wages goes out the window" [P. 123]. It is interesting to note that in *Value and Capital* Hicks [1946] admits to the possibility of instability in the factor market, but he does not follow up on the implication. In Chapter 8 he extends his theory of exchange to production and then looks at stability conditions, concluding that "it is still true that the only possible source of instability is strong asymmetry in income effects" [P. 103]. He then surveys four kinds of markets and suggests that any danger of instability will be concentrated in the factor market. He states,

10. See Samuelson's defense of the fairy tale on the flyleaf of Ferguson's text as well as Ferguson's defense on page 269.
11. See also Kaldor [1955–56], and note footnote 2 on page 89 for Wickstead's objection.

In the case of factor markets, a fall in price makes the supplier of the factor worse off, entrepreneurs better off; in view of the specialization of individuals on the provision of particular sorts of factors (so that, for example, employees do not usually provide the same sort of labour as their employers), this is particularly likely to leave a net income effect in the dangerous direction. [Ibid., p. 103]

Hicks was not interested in pursuing this line further because he then asked what the probability was of factor market instability extending to the system as a whole, and finally concluded that it is not likely [Ibid.]. This is important because a denial of the last question is not a denial of the existence of factor market instability. Yet Hicks is content to reason that while there may be more to say on the subject of stability, it is reasonable to assume a perfectly stable system of production equilibrium. And there the weight of established professional opinion remained until recent controversies in economics brought some old issues back into the foreground.

The most recent attack on marginal productivity theory has been launched in Cambridge, England.[12] As Joan Robinson has pointed out, the "neo-neoclassics," who attempted to reconstruct traditional orthodoxy after Keynes, took over Clark's definitions of capital, identified the rate of profit with the rate of interest, and maintained that the rate of profit received was due to the contribution of capital to output [1971, pp. 32-33].[13] Here we see Clark's distinction in capital becoming central to the argument. The Cambridge School maintains that the neo-neoclassics have consistently confused the concepts of capital that they used in their analysis. Or, put differently, current neoclassical economists interchange capital defined as a homogeneous fund with capital goods defined as a set of heterogeneous, disparate products. The point of all of this has been nicely summarized by Nell [1972]:

> Capital (homogeneous fund) is relevant to the analysis of the division of income among the members of society, but a non-specific fund has no bearing on production. Capital goods (heterogeneous set) are relevant to the study of production, but have no bearing on the distribution of income, since profit is earned and interest is paid, on the fund (value) of capital invested, regardless of its specific form. Capital goods can only be converted into a fund of capital on the basis of a given set of prices for those instruments; but to know these prices we must already know the general rate of profits (in a reason-

12. The single article best bringing the many threads of the "Cambridge controversy" together is Harcourt [1969].
13. Note particularly footnote 9 on p. 33.

ably competitive capitalist economy). Hence the amount of capital cannot be among the factors which set the level of the rate of profit. But in the orthodox, or neoclassical theory, the contribution of capital to production supposedly determines the rate of profit. This must be rejected. No sense can be given to the contribution to production of a fund of capital. [Pp. 40–41]

In other words, once we admit to the existence of heterogeneous capital, we have a problem with measurement of capital as a factor of production. The established way out of this problem is to value heterogeneous capital at current prices and then to sum up those values to arrive at a common monetary expression. But to do this involves circular reasoning. In order to determine these prices, one has to first assume a general rate of profit. Therefore, we run into the problem that if capital is to be treated as a sum of value, the values are not independent of the profit-wage rate to be determined. As Dobb [1970] states,

> Some defenders of orthodox doctrine seek to salvage certain propositions which they claim to be independent of any measurement of capital (such as Solow's recent attempt to give an unambiguous meaning to a 'social rate of return' on investment in a socialist system and to show that this must equal the rate of interest). But as Bhaduri and Pasinetti show in the September E.J., to invent a particular definition and to make what is defined equal to something else is to say nothing about how profit or rate of return is determined. [P. 4]

What does all of this mean for neoclassical economics? It means that once one assumes heterogeneous capital there may exist structure of production for which neoclassical results do not hold. Ferguson [1969] has capsulized the implication of the controversy quite well, as follows:

> If there is no scope for factor substitution except by switching from one fixed proportion process to another . . . a decrease in the rate of interest may be accompanied by a change from more to less capital-intensive methods of production. If so, there is not an invariant relation between the capital-labor ratio and the wage-rate of interest ratio. And if this invariant relation is missing . . . (out go) most of the theorems of simple neoclassical theory. [Pp. 254–255]

In essence, what the Cambridge Criticism has pointed out is that modern neoclassical theorists have assumed a priori a structure of production for which the neoclassical results hold when in fact there may exist structures of production where the relations do not hold. Ferguson, for one, admitted that the Cambridge Criticism is theoretically valid and that it may point to the Achilles heel of modern neoclassical economics:

> The full force of the Cambridge Criticism is as follows: it is illegiti-
> mate to make an *a priori* specification of the relations between the
> aggregate capital-labor ratio and the factor-price ratio; but more im-
> portantly still, it is even illegitimate to make such an *a priori* speci-
> fication for any sector of the economy. . . . Everything depends on
> the structure of production . . . if there is enough substitutability
> in the economy, either between factors of production or between
> commodities in demand, neoclassical theory emerges unscathed.
> Otherwise not. [Ibid., p. 258]

He goes on to add that if, in fact, the latter case holds, "Economists may be unable to make any statements concerning the relations of production to competitive input and output markets" [Ibid., p. 269]. This last statement is incorrect. What should have been said is that economists using the value perspective of the current neoclassical paradigm may be unable to make any statement about the relation of production to competitive input and output markets.

FROM THEORY TO PRACTICE

At this point one might ask, What has all this got to do with rural poverty? Many of the current interpretations and policy recommendations regarding poverty have their base in the current neoclassical paradigm. Although there now exists a vast literature on poverty and labor problems in general, the dominant analytical framework regards labor problems as a problem of market imperfection brought about by the "human" aspect of labor. The standard policy recommendations have been to suggest the enactment of some set of government programs to provide counseling, training, job information, moving expenses, etc., whereby the market imperfection associated with labor is corrected. But this whole approach assumes that the neoclassical relations hold once labor imperfections are corrected.

In light of the Cambridge Criticism, it is quite possible that this approach is in error. For if *the distribution of income cannot be explained in terms of marginal productivity theory, then "low-wage" poverty cannot be explained in terms of market efficiency.* The consequence of an untenable theory of distribution, as Joan Robinson has recently noted, places current economic orthodoxy in the position of having a "theory that cannot account

for the content of employment" [1972, p. 6]. The point here is not to deny
either the realities of market imperfection or the benefits to be derived from
government manpower programs. Rather, the issue is to point out the inadequacy of the value perspective of the current neoclassical paradigm as an
analytical framework for analyzing poverty. As one might guess, it is a philoso-
pher who has pointed to one of its major shortcomings:

> Economics as a separate science is unrealistic, and misleading if
> taken as a guide in practice. It is one element—a very important
> element, it is true—in a wider study, the science of power.
> [Bertrand Russell, quoted in Rothschild 1971, p. 7]

In summary, we now have, in addition to findings presented earlier
which do not square with marginal productivity theory, theoretical reasons
for questioning the applicability of marginal productivity theory in explaining
the agrarian revolution in the South. We are placed in the position of having to
rethink the problem. Accordingly, what follows is an attempt to draw together
into an alternative explanation the theoretical insights of a number of different
economists.

TOWARD A THEORY OF RURAL POVERTY[14]

Adolph Lowe [1965] has called attention to the fact that at any point in
time most of the firms have "money capital" sunk into a specific set of capital
goods [P. 237]. Further, unless amortization is fairly well advanced, it is going
to take several years for the mechanism of marginal productivity to work itself out [Ibid.]. This is not a problem as long as innovation is gradual and dis-
persed. However, under conditions where innovation is "bunched or clustered,"
displacement problems can arise. Under what type of technological change and
under what conditions are these problems likely to occur? When innovation is
"cost reducing"—by that Lowe means cheapening the output of existing products by reducing the factor input per unit of output—and when the factor input
reduced is labor, then innovation is labor-displacing [Ibid.]. Having established
the type of technology which is labor-displacing, Lowe then sets forth the conditions under which its effects may be "bunched or clustered."

> One might not go wrong in establishing the principle that a compen-
> sation problem, in the terms conceived by Ricardo and Marx, arises

14. The following discussion makes no claim to be a general theory of inequality.

mainly from two types of cost-reducing improvements; differential improvements of a very high productivity which create large and bunched displacement in marginal firms, and overall reorganization of whole industries which cause labor displacement even in the innovating firm. [Ibid., p. 241]

Finally, Lowe offers the following reservation regarding the homogeneity of labor. "Where displaced labor has a high degree of specificity the adjustment process of shifting labor is complicated and delayed" [Ibid., p. 244]. Interestingly enough, he does not push this point and feels that modern technology might favor "flexible skills" rather than rigid specialization. He concludes that if this is so, modern technology would facilitate the short-run adjustment process rather than impede it.

In general it is possible to "construct analytically certain cases in which positive and negative employment effects balance, especially by assuming several improvements occurring simultaneously in different industries," but as Lowe notes, "the conditions for such a balance are so complicated that they are practically irrelevant" [Ibid., p. 240].

Reder [1968], in his study of occupational wage differentials, raised the distributional question by asking what happens if economic change produces an increase in the work force which significantly exceeds the increase in aggregate demand for labor? While it is possible, a priori to construct models in which the excess labor supply is distributed across the various occupational skill groupings, the interesting case is that in which surplus labor is confined primarily to the low- and unskilled categories [Reder 1968]. It is particularly interesting because early nineteenth century English development establishes historical precedent for this case. Where development takes this form it puts extreme pressure on the lower classes by driving down "annual incomes of the unskilled, relative to the skilled, either by widening the per hour margin for skill or creating greater unemployment among the unskilled" [Ibid., p. 227]. The consequence is that even though a region or country may be experiencing economic growth, the lower classes are shut out from the benefits of economic progress. In other words, there is no good reason to assume, a priori, that the distribution of incremental increases in employment are proportional over the skill range. Where the distribution is unequal, then certain skill categories can experience severe economic hardship even though employment in the aggregate is increasing.

In brief, one can fit the facts of agricultural transformation in the South into a theoretical framework. Governmental intervention made it possible for a massive capitalization of Southern agriculture which not only displaced labor in marginal operations in the short-run but resulted in long-run structural reorganization which displaced labor in innovating operations. Further, the segments of Southern agriculture that bore the brunt of job losses were the low- and semi-skilled workers.

A full explanation of a structural transformation such as the one just described requires an excursion into the issue of power. Heilbroner has called our attention to the fact that a major shortcoming of neoclassical economics lies in its view of land, labor, and capital as purely neutral factors of production when in fact, labor, and capital are categories of social existence constituting a system of privilege [Heilbroner 1966]. The very operation of capitalism as a functioning system results in a pattern of wealth and income which in reality is a structural system of privilege. Similarly Rothschild has reminded us that people are not indifferent to the factors that affect their economic condition. Consequently it should be expected that "individuals and groups will struggle for position; that power will be used to improve one's chances in the economic 'game'; that attempts will be made to derive power and influence from acquired economic strongholds" [Rothschild 1971, p. 7].

The important idea here is that in viewing the factors of production as a system of privilege, one is also setting out a structure of economic and political power that groups can bring to bear to protect and/or improve their economic position. One of the more unusual value judgments implicit in neoclassical economics is in its theoretical formulation where

> ... more or less homogeneous units—firms and households—move in more or less given technological and market conditions and try to improve their economic lot *within the constraints of these conditions.* [Ibid.]

Ignored in such a formulation is the fact that groups may use power to change these constraints and in effect alter the outcome of market operations. [Ibid.] The suggestion here is not only that power can be used to alter market operations but more importantly that market operations will be more significantly altered the more unevenly power is distributed.

As I pointed out in Chapters 2 and 3, Southern agriculture has consistently displayed a pattern of economic and political inequality. While the general political climate in the thirties justified government intervention in agriculture, it was an agrarian power structure that gave the program its ultimate shape. To repeat from Chapter 3, one of the outstanding characteristics of agricultural transformation in the South has been the ability of the upper-income farmer to exercise political control over federal farm policy.

In other words, the key to understanding a socioeconomic transformation that has differential impact on the various classes in society lies in unevenly distributed economic and political power, in which some groups have sufficient power to protect or improve their position while others do not.

Now we can see the relevance of current debates in economic theory. In addition to the criticism just highlighted, marginal productivity theory is also hampered by the lack of a reliable theory of political decision-making. The merit of the Cambridge Criticism is not merely that it has pointed to problems with capital theory, income distribution, and the production function, but that it sees the limited applicability of neoclassical theory and the necessity of a new paradigm. To Cambridge Critics such matters as corporate power structure, unions, structure of industry, and politics should be included in the new paradigm. What the analysis in this study of agrarian transformation in the South points to is the *overriding necessity of beginning a new paradigm by first coming to grips with the nature and use of power, particularly political power.* In the South extended poverty has been the lot that befell those who did not possess sufficient economic and political power to protect and/or improve their position.

If we return to the classics, those authors would not find this argument startling. Neither Smith nor Marx would be taken aback by Heilbroner's suggestion that a system of privilege is inherent in a capitalist system. Marx particularly refined the classic concept of political power as a derivative of economic power. Given the "ban" on Marxian thought in the West, however, we are just now beginning to rediscover the insights of Marx and indeed of pre-Marxian classical political economy. Important as these insights are, they are still not sufficient. Western capitalism has gone through a massive transformation since Marx's day. It has changed from something like a competitive economy to an organized, controlled economy. While economic and political power are still interdependent, there is reason to suspect that "political power has begun to emancipate itself from its economic roots and, indeed, tends to become a base for the acquisition of economic power" [Neumann 1968].[15]

To fully understand rural poverty, however, it is necessary to look at the process by which a changing industrial mix in the nonagricultural sector also puts extreme pressure on redundant agrarian labor. It can only be through studied indifference to institutional realities that economists can assume that firms undertaking a training program would regard a thirty-seven-year-old ex-tenant farmer who does not speak the language very well as being identical to a recent high school graduate. Once labor markets are viewed as operating in

15. See also Heilbroner [1970, pp. 144–145].

some socioeconomic structural setting, there is little reason to assume that they will operate so as to alleviate poverty.

As was previously noted, Reder has suggested that economic growth can take a form in which some segments of society benefit while other segments are shut out. The work of Piore, Baron and Hymer, and Bluestone permit further development of the problem of market segmentation.

In Piore's [1971] view, socioeconomic transformation has led to a dual labor market. On the one hand, there exists a primary market offering employment opportunities with high wages, good working conditions, job security, etc. On the other, there exists a secondary market where employment is characterized by low wages, poor working conditions, and little opportunity for advancement. The significance of such a formulation is to point out that the poor are confined to the secondary market, and there is little chance of alleviating poverty unless they can enter primary employment. Access to primary employment will be difficult since the poor do participate in the economy and have economic value where they are; consequently, groups exist which not only will reject poverty programs but will actually benefit from the perpetuation of poverty [Ibid.].

The issue here is not one of simple wage exploitation, although that may indeed occur. Bluestone's [1971] study of marginal industries found that low-wage industries could be characterized as having below-average levels of absolute productivity, less capital, smaller profits, and extensive competition. In contrast to industries that are capital-intense, highly profitable, and oligopolistic in structure, there is serious doubt about the ability of low-wage industries to pay adequate wages without drastically curtailing employment. In other words, the working poor are not being exploited by individual firms as much as by structural characteristics of the economy as a whole.

Here we get to the heart of the matter. At issue is an explanation of how simultaneous structural change in both the agricultural sector and the nonagricultural sector has operated so as to lock a significant segment of our working population into the secondary employment sector.

The outstanding characteristic of the industrial revolution and the rise of the manufacturing system was the subdividing of the production process into an organized number of simple, repetitive steps so that essentially low-skilled labor could produce complex products. Increased productivity could be had by increased specialization subject to the limitations of the market. Clark and Marshall, as well as the Austrian School in general, would admit to long-run changes in the pattern of production but foresaw no problem because they all assumed that "the outstanding trend will be toward an increasing importance of the production of capital goods" as far as the employment of labor is concerned [Gourvitch 1966].

An increasing proportion of the labor force will be shifted to the production of [producers'] goods. All this will be designed to provide an increasing flow of finished goods and an ever more abundant consumption as time goes on. [Ibid., p. 102]

The outstanding trend in the post-World War II period has been the rise of the service economy. Employment in manufacturing has been relatively stable, with service and government providing the major opportunities for employment. To get at the consequences of a changing industrial mix on employment, it is necessary to define labor and capital in terms of production and then ask three questions: What shifts in employment have taken place between occupations at both the national and regional level? Second, what shifts in employment have taken place between sectors within regions? Third, within each sector what shifts in employment have occurred in response to changing skill requirements for the new positions created?

Let us take up these questions in reverse order. To make the argument explicit, an example will first be presented from Burstein's [1968] study of New York City, whose data on labor and capital is consistent with definitions used here. The analysis will then be extended to Appalachia.

Between 1950 and 1967, New York City's industrial mix underwent considerable change with "goods-producing" industries declining in importance relative to the "service-producing" sector in terms of employment. Employment declined by 193,000 jobs in the goods-producing sector, with the decline being concentrated in construction and manufacturing. In the same period, employment in the service-producing sector rose sufficiently to cover those losses and to add an additional 202,000 jobs to the city's total. Within the service sector employment gains were as follows:

Service and Misc.	213,700
Government	131,000
Finance-Ins.-Real.	72,000 [Ibid., p. 2]

To conclude that there has been a significant improvement in the employment picture for New York is relatively meaningless until the distribution of those jobs over the skill range is known. Burstein has computed the ratio of semi- and low-skilled workers employed for each 100 workers employed in each sector. Here are the results:

Manufacturing	66
Service and Misc.	42
Government	35
Finance-Ins.-Real.	19 [Ibid., p. 6]

If for the moment we hold these ratios constant and the composition of the labor force constant, we can work with the consequences of changing industrial mix. A shift of 100 jobs from manufacturing to service would reduce the employment of semi- and low-skilled workers by 24; a shift to government of 100 jobs would reduce such employment by 31; and a shift to finance and insurance would reduce such employment by 47 jobs. Or, as Burstein notes:

> To provide enough low skilled jobs to replace 100 manufacturing jobs it would be necessary to generate 150 new positions in the division of services and misc., or 200 government jobs, or as many as 350 in finance, or some combination of all three. [Ibid.]

The above statement only defines what is needed to *maintain* the existing level of employment in low-skilled ranks. To lower the unemployment rate for the low-skilled, the increase in jobs in the service-producing sector would have to be still higher. If we drop the assumptions of a constant labor force (permitting the mix of labor skills to change adversely) and a constant ratio of semi- and low-skilled to total employment (permitting the possibility of technology to lower the amount of low-skilled labor employed), the increase in the service sector would be even higher. This led Burstein to conclude that "increases in total employment in the City would have to be of a high (maybe impossible) order of magnitude, if they are to result in further substantial reductions in the number of the unemployed" [Ibid., p. 9].

While Burstein does not elaborate as to why it may be impossible the answer is fairly obvious. Any community whose growth industries lie in the service sector and which is faced with the task of absorbing sizable numbers of semi-skilled workers cannot generate a rate of investment sufficient to provide adequate employment for the lower skilled. Further, it presents a problem for macro policy designed to aid employment through increased investment. A country experiencing a structural transformation whereby growth in employment is primarily in the service sector may not be able to provide a rate of investment sufficient to provide adequate income employment for the low-skilled and still maintain price stability. There is little evidence to support the position that monetary and fiscal policy are implemented in a socially neutral fashion. Where the trade-off is between, first, monetary and fiscal policy beneficial to established economic interests and, second, an increase in unemployment for the lower skilled, the tendency seems to be opting for increased unemployment and explaining away the consequences in terms of individual failure on the part of the lower classes.

When we turn to Appalachia, the same general picture appears. Between 1950 and 1960 the technological revolution in agriculture and mining reduced employment by 600,000 (see Table 4–4). Further, workers displaced were primarily in the low-skilled range. Employment in the nonagricultural sector rose by 568,000, leaving in the aggregate a deficit of 32,000 jobs. A closer look at the data reveals that the labor displacement problem was much more severe. The goods-producing sector, the major user of low-skilled labor, increased employment by 226,000 jobs. However, the biggest increase in employment occurred in the service-producing sector. But 237,000 jobs, or 75 percent of the total employment increase in the service sector, according to U.S. Department of Agriculture [1965] figures, occurred in professional-technical, finance-insurance, and public administration, areas which are *not* a source of employment for submarginal farmers and coal miners. In fact, slightly over 50 percent (169,000) of the total job increase in the service-producing sector was in the professional-technical categories alone [Ibid.]. Viewed in this light, growth of employment in the nonagricultural sector could at best provide employment opportunities for about half of those displaced out of agriculture and mining. It is this fundamental shift in sectors, with their differential impact on labor, rather than Appalachian culture that gives rise to poverty. Further, recent action by the Labor Department suggests that the rural manpower program has been of limited benefit to date. Specifically, the Labor Department recently announced reorganization of its rural manpower program after a departmental study indicated that the existing programs seemed to be facilitating the interests of employers rather than servicing labor as it had originally been designed to do [Shabecoff 1972].

Table 4–4. Employment Changes in Appalachia: 1950–1960

Sectors	Changes in Jobs (000)	
Agricultural sector	−223.9	
Mining sector	−265.4	
Total		−600.3
Nonagriculture sector:		
Goods–producing	226.7	
Service–producing	341.4	
Total		568.1
Total change in jobs		−32.0

Source: U.S. Dept. of Agriculture, 1965, pp. 41, 53, 67.

THE CASE AGAINST MANAGED
AGGREGATE DEMAND

Modern Keynesians are not particularly sympathetic to technological unemployment. For the, the problem lies with discrepancy between planned savings and planned investment. Perhaps Heller [1965] gives the most concise statement in this regard. While he admits that problems of structural unemployment exist, he claims that these problems are not new nor have they suddenly become more serious. "The expansion of total demand through tax reduction remains the crucial central element in our attack upon unemployment" [Ibid., p. 140]. The problem is primarily one of aggregate demand. Once government policy has established a satisfactory level of aggregate demand we can rely on the "proven capacity of a free labor market . . . to reconcile discrepancies between particular labor supplies and particular labor demands" [Ibid., p. 137]. Here it is hard to distinguish between Heller and neoclassical economics.

> If relative shortages of particular skills develop, the price system and the market will moderate them, as they always have done in the past. Employers will be prompted to step up their in-service training programs and, as more jobs become available, poorly skilled and poorly educated workers will be more strongly motivated to avail themselves of training, retraining, and adult education opportunities. Government manpower programs begun in 1961–63 period will also be operating to help ease the adjustment of specific skill shortages. [Ibid.]

With regard to this last assertion it is only necessary to point to the analysis above and the findings of Hathaway and Perkins. Rather than belabor that argument further, let us look more closely at Heller's basic argument that the matter is primarily one of managed aggregate demand.

First, note the particular formulation of the technological unemployment argument. By formulating the technological unemployment argument as a "structural bottleneck," making it impossible to achieve a 4 percent unemployment rate, then the test of such a formulation is whether the economy can grow at a rate sufficient to reduce unemployment to a level of 4 percent. If so, we dismiss structural unemployment as a problem. The possibility of people being factored out in the process of economic growth is simply not considered. This formulation of the problem is essentially the same as Clark's: "There is no larger proportion of the laboring population in idleness now than there was at the beginning of the period" [1899, pp. 258-259]. But as I have argued throughout this analysis, this formulation misses the point. One has to look at the distribution of costs and benefits of economic growth. Further, constancy in aggregate labor share does not establish that all is well because it fails to reveal the *redistribution within labor.* For that matter, aggregative measures of business income and property income are subject to the same limitation.

To fully understand the limitations of modern Keynesian aggregative formulations, it is necessary to look at changes in employment over time at both the national and regional level. If we begin by looking at Table 4-5, a number of trends are observable.

1. In the postwar period the significant rise in employment was in the white-collar and service categories. More specifically, note that the most significant change in the white-collar category was in the professional-technical and kindred workers.
2. The farm sector showed the expected decline with employment being almost halved by 1964.
3. The blue-collar sector exhibited a very low growth rate. In fact, from 1951 to 1964 it was virtually constant.

Thus, the impact of structural transformation on employment in the U.S. economy was at the extreme ends of the skill range with the blue-collar sector, the major source of employment for the semi- and low-skilled labor holding constant. This shift is important. Modern economists have pointed to the expanding employment in the service sector as proof that Marx was wrong, that there was no increase in the "reserve army of the unemployed." This dismissal may have ignored the structural problem that was rising, i.e., that huge amounts of semi- and low-skilled labor were being pushed out of the agricultural sector into the nonagricultural sector, while at the same time the major expansion in the nonagricultural sector was in the service-producing sector—*the sector which employs the lowest proportion of semi- and low-skilled labor as compared to the goods-producing sector.*

In Table 4-6 we can look at this structural transformation in regional terms. Again we see that the general pattern holds, with large declines in agricultural employment, major increases in employment in the white-collar occupations, and blue-collar employment exhibiting low rates of growth. This is especially true for the South because of its large agrarian base and relatively small industrial base. The degree of dislocation varied from region to region depending upon the socioeconomic structure of the region in question. In the South with its large peasant-based agriculture,[16] small industrial base and pecu-

16. See Conrad [1965] for an interesting argument for treating Southern agriculture as a "peasant-based" agricultural system.

Table 4-5. Employed Persons by Occupation, Annual Averages, 1947–1964

Year	Total Em-ployed	White-Collar					Blue-Collar				Service			Farm Workers		
		Total	Prof. Tech. Kind.	M'grs Office Prop's Kind.	Cleric Kind.	Sales Kind.	Total	Craft. Fore-men	Opera-tives Kind.	Labor Excl. Farm	Total	Pri-vate House	Serv. Excl. P.House	Total	Farm Owner M'gr	Farm Labor
	(000)															
1947	57,843	20,185	3,795	5,795	7,200	3,295	23,554	7,754	12,274	3,526	5,987	1,731	4,256	8,120	4,995	3,125
1951	60,854	22,413	4,788	6,220	7,655	3,750	25,009	8,434	12,623	3,952	6,533	1,869	4,664	6,900	4,025	2,875
1964	70,357	31,125	8,550	7,452	10,667	4,456	25,534	8,986	12,924	3,624	9,256	2,322	6,934	4,444	2,320	2,124
	(%)															
1947	100.0	34.9	6.6	10.0	12.4	5.9	40.7	13.4	21.2	6.1	10.4	3.0	7.4	14.0	8.6	5.4
1951	100.0	36.8	7.9	10.2	12.6	6.2	41.1	13.9	20.7	6.5	10.8	3.1	7.7	11.3	6.6	4.7
1964	100.0	44.2	12.2	10.6	15.2	6.3	36.3	12.8	18.4	5.2	13.2	3.3	9.9	6.3	3.3	3.0

Source: U.S. President, 1965, pp. 202–203.

Table 4-6. Percentage Change in Employment, by Major Occupational Group: 1950–1960

Major Occupational Group	Total	New Eng.	Atla.	East North Cen.	West North Cen.	South Atla.	East South Cen.	West South Cen.	Mtn.	Pacf.
All occupations	10.4	6.7	5.6	7.9	1.8	14.9	-0.5	9.7	30.8	33.4
Prof.–tech.	47.0	41.6	35.0	41.9	35.5	57.7	40.2	47.5	73.6	75.0
Farmers & mgrs.	-41.9	-46.5	-36.0	-35.9	-27.9	-50.7	-55.2	-53.2	-33.2	-29.9
Mgrs.–officials	7.4	-0.7	-5.8	1.0	(?)	24.3	10.8	14.9	35.0	20.7
Clerical, kind.	33.8	25.3	22.6	25.1	25.1	46.6	38.1	42.6	68.7	61.3
Sales workers	18.7	10.1	14.5	15.9	8.7	30.2	17.3	16.9	35.8	30.5
Crafts, fore.	11.8	6.9	-1.8	6.1	4.7	23.0	17.1	16.3	36.0	28.4
Operative, kind.	6.4	-6.2	-4.9	1.9	10.8	10.6	13.2	23.1	30.5	34.1
Priv. household	22.3	5.7	1.8	23.3	36.6	20.7	25.6	29.0	72.4	50.6
Service workers	26.7	19.3	15.8	22.7	28.3	36.8	27.6	32.0	54.2	35.0
Farm laborers	-40.2	-36.2	-38.6	-43.2	-48.7	-41.2	-45.3	-44.3	-29.2	-14.6
Labor, ex. Farm	-9.6	-19.8	-16.7	-9.0	-18.6	-5.2	-6.5	-9.3	6.2	1.6

Source: U.S. President, 1965, p. 274.

liar sociopolitical structure, the impact of economic change was catastrophic for the lower classes. While it can be argued that higher aggregate demand would raise employment levels, there is no reason to believe that the incremental increase in employment will be proportional across the skill range, or that stimulation to aggregate demand would not speed up structural transformation.

Table 4-7 is quite revealing in this regard. Unemployment rates are broken down by occupational class. The combined effect of the Heller tax cut and huge federal deficits produced by the war never reduced unemployment below 4.4 percent for the operative category and never below 6.7 percent in the unskilled labor category. When allowances are made for the fact that unemployment excludes those who are no longer looking for a job, makes no allowance for underemployment, or considers the income level of the employed, the magnitude of the problem of adequate income for the lower skilled in our society is significantly raised. Average national unemployment rates of 4 percent or less were achieved through extremely low unemployment rates in the white-collar class. Note particularly the tight market in professional-technical and managerial-official categories.

CONCLUSIONS

The rise of pure theory in economics resulted in a fundamental methodological transformation from that employed by classical economists. Instead of a model of a particular socioeconomic system, the intent was to establish a set of general principles which would hold independent of time, place, and environment [Lowe 1965]. To do this it was necessary to isolate an economic core process which one could manipulate under a set of assumed conditions. This isolation, however, necessitated setting aside the following:

> ... involvement with the structure and evolution of a distinctive society; commitment to a particular welfare goal; and last but not least, adoption of a specific motivational pattern. [Ibid., pp. 194–195]

The results were to transform economics into the science of conditional analysis. When asked about the economy, the economist replies: "I don't know; but if the set of conditions A holds, then such and such will happen. On the other hand, if this set of conditions B, holds, then. . . . " Therein lies the problem. We have a catalog with varying sets of conditions, but we do not know

Table 4-7. Unemployment Rates of Persons Sixteen Years and Over and Percentage Distribution of Unemployment by Occupational Group, Annual Average: 1958-1970

		White-Collar					Blue-Collar			
Year	Total Unemp.	Total	Prof. Tech.	Mgrs. Props.	Cler. Workers	Sales Workers	Total	Craft. Fore.	Oper.	Non-farm Labor
1958	6.8	3.1	2.0	1.7	4.4	4.1	10.2	6.8	11.0	15.0
1959	5.5	2.6	1.7	1.3	3.7	3.8	7.6	5.3	7.6	12.6
1960	5.5	2.7	1.7	1.4	3.8	3.8	7.8	5.3	8.0	12.6
1961	6.7	3.3	2.0	1.8	4.6	4.9	9.2	6.3	9.6	14.7
1962	6.6	2.8	1.7	1.5	4.0	4.3	7.4	5.1	7.5	12.5
1963	5.7	2.9	1.8	1.5	4.0	4.3	7.3	4.8	7.5	12.4
1964	5.2	2.6	1.7	1.4	3.7	3.5	6.3	4.1	6.6	10.8
1965	4.5	2.3	1.5	1.1	3.3	3.4	5.3	3.6	5.5	8.6
1966	3.8	2.0	1.3	1.0	2.9	2.8	4.2	2.2	4.4	7.4
1967	3.8	2.2	1.3	.9	3.1	3.2	4.4	2.5	5.0	7.6
1968	3.6	2.0	1.2	1.0	3.0	2.8	4.1	2.4	4.5	7.2
1969	3.5	2.1	1.3	.9	3.0	2.9	3.9	2.2	.4.4	6.7
1970	4.9	2.8	3.0	1.3	4.0	3.9	6.2	3.8	7.1	9.5

Source: U.S. President, 1971, p. 222.

beforehand which set of conditions will hold or whether our catalog even contains the appropriate set of conditions.[17]

The price mechanism in modern neoclassical theory is assigned a double task. First, it is supposed to provide a rate of privately generated new capital formation sufficient to provide full employment. Second, the price mechanism is to allocate labor according to its marginal product and to reallocate any labor dislocated by the introduction of new technology. In contrast to these assumptions, it is the finding of this study that the flow of investment and technology in the farm sector has primarily been in response to *public subsidy* and that labor market reallocation of displaced labor has been *perverse*.

It is one thing to ask whether an economic model is logically consistent under a given set of assumptions, and quite another to ask whether a model makes any sense in explaining actual economic events. In this regard marginal productivity theory suffers serious shortcomings. The work of Lowe and the Cambridge School show clearly that marginal productivity theory holds under a specific set of conditions, and once these conditions are violated the theory breaks down as an explanation of production and distribution.

17. This line of reasoning was first suggested in a lecture given by Lowe at the New School for Social Research in the fall of 1969.

The Cambridge School has taken a significant step toward the reformulation of theory by constructing models in which perfect competition and profit maximization are not essential conditions, as well as a savings function which is much more realistic than the orthodox assumptions. However, Cambridge formulations still suffer limitations. The first limitation is the level of aggregation, which leaves the differential impact of change within regions and sectors unanalyzed. This is not a fatal objection since eventual disaggregation could accommodate Cambridge models to the task. Second, Cambridge Critics have failed to come to grips with the fact that "labor" is just as fictitious an entity as "capital." Consequently, labor in most Cambridge formulations is still an undifferentiated, unanalyzed mass of workers. Third, and quite serious, is the absence of a public sector. The absence of government from marginal productivity theory and Cambridge formulations leaves a major variable outside their analyses.[18] Rural poverty in the South can be explained more readily in political terms than in terms of efficiency. The demise of the family farm in the fifties and sixties is more the consequence of its inability to compete with large subsidized operations than it is any basic inefficiency.

Leontief [1958] concluded a short theoretical essay on "Time-Preference, Productivity of Capital, Stagnation, and Economic Growth" with the observation that further theoretical speculations of this kind were subject to diminishing returns. "The effort in construction and interpretation of more complicated graphs might better be spent on observation and explanation of the real world" [P. 111]. And so it is with the current state of economic theory as it relates to an analysis of poverty.

The essential findings of this study are that at the macro level the rural poor are trapped by simultaneous structural change in both the agricultural and nonagricultural sectors of our economy. In the agricultural sector, a politically biased government subsidy program has permitted the larger commercial farmer to integrate new capital and new technology into his farming operation, thereby displacing large quantities of low-skilled workers to be absorbed by the nonagricultural sector. However, structural change in the nonagricultural sector constrained employment opportunities for low-skilled labor. In goods-producing industries—the major user of low-skilled labor—employment remained virtually constant from 1951 to 1964. (The short-lived spurt in employment occurring in manufacturing from 1965 to 1969 would appear to be primarily in response to defense buildup associated with the war.)

The major growth in employment has occurred in the service-producing sector—a sector that uses relatively small amounts of low-skilled labor.

---

18. This limitation has been acknowledged by Harcourt [1965].

The results, as Minsky has pointed out, are a set of economic conditions in which *substantial economic growth could take place without significant reduction in the number of rural poor.* As long as there is a surplus of low-skilled labor coming out of the rural sector, the urban sector can regard its supply curve of low-wage labor as infinitely elastic at a supply price at or near a poverty level of existence. The primary result of economic growth, then, is to shift labor from rural poverty to urban poverty.

It is the micro level that one can most easily see the tragic consequences for rural communities caught in this transformation process.

1. Massive technological innovation in Southern agriculture displaced large quantities of low-skilled labor for the nonagricultural sector to absorb.
2. Rural communities of the South, in which the nonagricultural sector was either small or nonexistent, had limited capacity for growth.
3. Labor market realloclation of redundant labor has been perverse, from the standpoint of the sending rural communities—with only the younger, higher skilled, better educated being able to make the transition.
4. A persistent realloclation pattern of this type produces severe adverse consequences for those who remain: (a) the community incurs the burden of a relatively high dependency ratio; (b) over time there is a tendency for the composition of dependency ratio to shift as the percentage of persons over 65 increases relative to those under 18; (c) the earnings base of the community is eroded as the index of skills and age turns unfavorable to the community.
5. The consequence for local community government is not only higher per capita overhead but is a reduced tax base for provisioning the public sector.
6. Deterioration in the public sector, whether relative or absolute, results not only in a general inability of the community to provide for its own needs but makes it increasingly difficult for the community to alter the path of stagnation and decay on its own initiative.
7. For the young who by the accident of birth are born into these communities, the problem of transition becomes increasingly difficult. High school graduates who have the equivalency rate of eighth grade achievement in English, math, and science are virtually denied an effective place in modern industrial society. The tasks of overcoming these deficiences are difficult in their own right, but to the individual who is poor the task of overcoming these deficiencies without economic resources at his disposal requires an unusual degree of personal perseverance.
8. The major distinction that can be drawn between white and black rural poverty, as represented by Appalachia and the Core South, is that racial discrimination has made the transition for blacks even more difficult.

It is unfortunate that the social sciences have spent most of the last
ten years in studies of poverty with emphasis on the individual or culture, rather
than in terms of the impact that macro structure could have in a changing
economic environment. The consequence was a fundamental misdirection.
Cultural peculiarities are not the cause of poverty, they are a link in the chain
of causes. It is the inequitable distribution of gains and losses from economic
change that lies at the heart of the poverty problem. The upper-income farmer
has been able to insulate himself from the pressures of the market through
public subsidy over the last thirty-five years. In direct contrast to the prevailing public belief as to how the system operated, an agricultural system arose
that provided welfare for the rich and the market system for the poor. The
alleviation of rural poverty will remain an unfulfilled hope as long as this set
of political privileges remains intact.

References

Agee, James, and Evans, Walker. 1939, 1960 *Let Us Now Praise Famous Men.* New York: Ballentine Books.

Ball, Richard A. 1970. "The Southern Appalachian Folk Subculture as a Tension Reducing Way of Life." In *Change in Rural Appalachia: Implications for Action Programs,* edited by J. Photiadis and H. Schwarzweller, pp. 69–79. Philadelphia: Univ. of Pennsylvania Press.

Baumol, William J. 1967. "Macroeconomics of Unbalanced Growth: The Anatomy of the Urban Crisis." *American Economic Review* 57: 152–159.

Bluestone, Barry. 1971. "The Characteristics of Marginal Industries." In *Problems in Political Economy: An Urban Perspective,* edited by D. Gordon, pp. 102–107. Lexington, Mass.: D.C. Heath.

Bonnen, James T. 1968. "Distribution of Benefits from Selected Farm Programs." In U.S. President's National Advisory Commission on Rural Poverty, *Rural Poverty in the United States,* pp. 461–505. Washington, D.C.: U.S. Government Printing Office.

Brown, James S. 1970. "Population and Migration Change in Appalachia." In *Change in Rural Appalachia: Implications for Action Programs,* edited by J. Photiadis and H. Schwarzweller, pp. 23–49. Philadelphia: Univ. of Pennsylvania Press.

Bryan, Hobson C., and Bertrand, Alvin L. 1970. *The Propensity for Change Among the Rural Poor in the Mississippi Delta.* U.S. Department of Agriculture, Economic Research Service, Agriculture Economic Report No. 185. Washington, D.C.: U.S. Government Printing Office.

Burstein, Abraham C. 1968. *Manpower Problems in New York City.* Rev. ed. New York: New York City Human Resources Administration, Division of Planning, Research, and Evaluation.

Campbell, Christiana M. 1962. *The Farm Bureau.* Urbana: Univ. of Illinois Press.

Cash, W. J. 1941. *The Mind of the South.* New York: Random House.

Caudill, Harry M. 1963. *Night Comes to the Cumberlands.* Boston: Little, Brown.

Christenson, Reo M. 1959. *The Brannan Plan: Farm Politics and Policy.* Ann Arbor: Univ. of Michigan Press.

Clark, Kenneth B. 1965. *Dark Ghetto: Dilemmas of Social Power.* New York: Harper and Row.

Clark, J. B. 1899. *The Distribution of Wealth.* London: Macmillan. 1968. *Essentials of Economic Theory.* New York: Augustus M. Kelley.

Coltrane, R. I., and Blaum, E. I. 1965. *An Economic Survey of the Appalachia Region.* U.S. Department of Agriculture, Economic Research Service, Agriculture Economic Report No. 69. Washington, D.C.: U.S. Government Printing Office.

Conrad, David E. 1965. *The Forgotten Farmer: The Story of Share Croppers in the New Deal.* Urbana: Univ. of Illinois Press.

Cooper, William H. 1968. "A Clinical Economist in Rural Poverty." *American Economic Review Papers and Proceedings* 58: 321–327.

Day, Richard H. 1967. "The Economics of Technological Change and the Demise of the Sharecropper." *American Economic Review* 57: 427–449.

Dobb, Maurice. 1970. Some Reflections on the Sraffa System and the Critique of the So-Called Neo-Classical Theory of Value and Distribution. Paper submitted at the Conference of Socialist Economists, London, January 1970.

Dunbar, Tony. 1971. *Our Land Too.* New York: Random House.

Dunn, F. 1962. *Recent Southern Economic Development. As Revealed by Changing Structure of Employment.* Gainesville: Univ. of Florida.

Ferguson, C. E. 1969. *The Neoclassical Theory of Production and Distribution.* Cambridge: Cambridge Univ. Press.

Ford, Thomas R., ed. 1962. *The Southern Appalachian Region: A Survey.* Lexington: Univ. of Kentucky Press.

Ford, Thomas R., and Hillery, George A. 1968. "Rural Community Institutions, with Special Reference to Health and Education." In U.S. President's National Advisory Commission on Rural Poverty, *Rural Poverty in the United States,* pp. 74–85. Washington, D. C.: U.S. Government Printing Office.

Friedman, Rose. 1965. *Poverty: Definition and Perspective.* Washington, D.C.: American Enterprise Institute for Public Policy Research.

Fulmer, John. L. 1950. *Agriculture Progress in the Cotton Belt Since 1920.* Chapel Hill: Univ. of North Carolina Press.

Gourvitch, Alexander. 1966. *Survey of Economic Theory on Technological Change and Employment.* New York: Augustus M. Kelley.

Haber, A. 1966. "Poverty Budgets: How Much Is Enough." *Poverty and Human Resources Abstracts.* vol. 1, no. 3.

Harcourt, G. C. 1965. "Two Sector Model of the Distribution and the Level of Employment in the Short-Run." *Economic Record* 41: 103–117.

1969. "Some Cambridge Controversies in the Theory of Capital." *Journal of Economic Literature* 7: 369–405.

Hardin, C. 1946. "The Bureau of Agricultural Economics Under Fire." *Journal of Farm Economics* 28: 635–668.

Harrington, Michael. 1962. *The Other America: Poverty in the U.S.* New York: Macmillan.

Hathaway, Dale E., and Perkins, Brian E. 1968. "Occupational Mobility and Migration from Agriculture." In U.S. President's National Advisory Commission on Rural Poverty, *Rural Poverty in the United States,* pp. 185–237. Washington, D.C.: U.S. Government Printing Office.

Heilbroner, Robert L. 1966. *Limits of American Capitalism.* New York: Harper and Row. 1970. *Between Capitalism and Socialism: Essays in Political Economics.* New York: Random House.

Heller, Walter. 1965. "The Case for Aggregate Demand." In *The Manpower Revolution,* edited by G. Mangum, pp. 117–146. Garden City: Doubleday.

Herr, William McD. 1968. "Credit and Farm Policy." In U.S. President's National Advisory Commission on Rural Poverty, *Rural Poverty in the United States.* pp. 522–641. Washington, D.C.: U.S. Government Printing Office.

Johnson, Harry G. 1970. "Planning and the Market in Economic Development." In *Economic Development: Readings in Theory and Practice,* edited by T. Morgan and G. Betz, pp. 289–299. Belmont, Calif.: Wadsworth.

Kain, John F., and Persky, Joseph J. 1968. "The North's Stake in Southern Rural Poverty." In U.S. President's National Advisory Commission on Rural Poverty, *Rural Poverty in the United States,* pp. 288–308. Washington, D.C.: U.S. Government Printing Office.

Kaldor, Nicholas. 1955–56. "Alternative Theories of Distribution." *Review of Economic Studies* 23: 83–100. 1959–60. "A Rejoinder to Mr. Atsumi and Professor Tobin." *Review of Economic Studies* 27: 121–123.

Keynes, J.M. 1965. *The General Theory of Employment, Interest, and Money.* New York: Harcourt, Brace & World.

Kile, Orville. 1921. *The Farm Bureau Movement.* New York: Macmillan. 1948. *The Farm Bureau Through the Decades.* Baltimore: Waverly Press.

Leontief, Wassily. 1958. "Theoretical Note on Time Preference, Productivity of Capital, Stagnation, and Economic Growth." *American Economic Review* 48: 105–111.

Lowe, Adolph. 1954. "The Classical Theory of Economic Growth." *Social Research* 21: 121–158. 1965. *On Economic Knowledge.* New York: Harper and Row. n.d. *Technological Unemployment Reexamined.* Zurich: Eugen Rentsch Verlag Erlenback.

Lustig, Morton, and Reiner, Janet S. 1968. "Local Government and Poverty in Rural Areas." In U.S. President's National Advisory Commission on Rural Poverty, *Rural Poverty in the United States.* Washington, D.C.: U.S. Government Printing Office.

Marshall, F. Ray. 1972. "Some Rural Economic Development in the South." *American Economic Review Paper and Proceedings* 62: 204–211.

Marx, Karl. 1909. *Capital.* Vol. III. Chicago: C.H. Kerr.

McConnell, Grant. 1953. *The Decline of Agrarian Democracy.* Berkeley: Univ. of California Press.

McCune, Wesley. 1956. *Who's Behind Our Farm Policy.* New York: Praeger.

Merton, Robert S. 1968. *Social Theory and Social Structure.* New York: Free Press.

Miller, Herman P. 1971. *Rich Man, Poor Man.* New York: Thomas Y. Crowell.

Mills, C. Wright. 1960. *Images of Man.* New York: Braziller.

Minsky, Human P. 1968. "Adequate Aggregate Demand and a Commitment to End Poverty." In U.S. President's National Advisory Commission on Rural Poverty, *Rural Poverty in the United States,* pp. 562–580. Washington, D.C.: U.S. Government Printing Office.

Myrdal, Gunnar. 1944. *An American Dilemma.* New York: Harper and Row.

Nell, Edward J. 1972. "The Revival of Political Economy." *Social Research* 39: 32–52.

Neumann, Franz L. 1968. "Approaches to the Study of Political Power." In *Comparative Politics: Notes and Readings,* edited by R. Macridis and B. Brown, pp. 67–75. 3rd ed. Homewood, Ill.: Dorsey.

Orshansky, Mollie. 1968. "Counting the Poor: Another Look at the Poverty Profile." In *Poverty in America,* edited by L. Ferman et al., pp. 67–106. Ann Arbor: Univ. of Michigan Press.

Orwell, George. 1961. *The Road to Wigan Pier.* New York: Berkley.

Perelman, Michael. 1971. "Second Thoughts on the Green Revolution." *New Republic* 165: 21–22.

Piore, Michael. 1971. "The Dual Labor Market: Theory and Implications." In *Problems in Political Economy: An Urban Perspective,* edited by D. Gordon, pp. 90–94. Lexington, Mass.: D.C. Heath.

Raup, Philip M. 1967. "Land Reform and Agricultural Development." In *Agricultural Development and Economic Growth,* edited by H.M. Southworth and B.F. Johnston, pp. 267–314. Ithaca: Cornell.

Reder, M.W. 1968. "The Theory of Occupational Wage Differentials." In *The Labour Market,* edited by B. McCormick and E. Smith, pp. 203–207. Baltimore: Penguin Books.

Rein, Martin. 1968. "Problems in the Definition and Measurement of Poverty." In *Poverty in America,* edited by L. Ferman et al., pp. 116–133. Ann Arbor: Univ. of Michigan Press.

Ricardo, David. 1911. *Principles of Political Economy and Taxation.* 3rd ed. London: J.M. Dent and Sons.

Robinson, Joan. 1947. *An Essay on Marxian Economics.* London: Macmillan. 1971. *Economic Heresies: Some Old-Fashioned Questions in Economic Theory.* New York: Basic Books.

Rohrer, Wayne C., and Douglas, Louis H. 1969. *The Agrarian Transition in America: Dualism and Change.* Indianapolis: Bobbs-Merrill.

Rothschild, K.W., ed. 1971. *Power in Economics.* Baltimore: Penguin Books.

Rousseau, Jean Jacques. 1952. *Discourse on the Origins of Inequality.* Chicago: Encyclopedia Britannica.

Ruttan, Vernon W. 1966. "Agricultural Policy in an Affluent Society." *Journal of Farm Economics* 48: 1100–1130.

Schuh, G. Edward. 1968. "Interrelationship Between the Farm Labor Force and Changes in the Total Economy." In U.S. President's National Advisory Commission on Rural Poverty, *Rural Poverty in the United States,* pp. 170–184. Washington, D.C.: U.S. Government Printing Office.

Schultz, Theodore W. 1949. *Production and Welfare of Agriculture.* New York: Macmillan.

Schultze, Charles. 1972. "The Distribution of Farm Subsidies." In *Redistribution to the Rich and the Poor: The Grants Economics of Income Distribution,* edited by K. Boulding and M. Pfaff, pp. 94–116. Belmont, Calif.: Wadsworth.

Schwarzweller, Harry K. 1970. "Social Change and the Individual." In *Change in Rural Appalachia: Implications for Action Programs,* edited by J. Photiadis and H. Schwarzweller, pp. 51–68. Philadelphia: Univ. of Pennsylvania Press.

Shabecoff, P. 1972. "U.S. Farm Agency Reported to Foster Abuse of Migrants." *New York Times,* 23 April, 1972, pp. 1, 29.

Slocum, Walter. 1967. *Aspirations and Expectations of the Rural Poor.* U.S. Department of Agriculture, Economic Research Service, Economic Research Bulletin No. 122. Washington, D.C.: U.S. Government Printing Office.

Steinbeck, John. 1941. *Grapes of Wrath.* New York: Modern Library.

U.S. Bureau of the Census. 1964. *Agriculture Census, 1964,* Vol. 2. Washington, D.C.: U.S. Government Printing Office.

U.S. Congress, *Congressional Record,* 89th Cong., 1st Sess., 1965, 111, pt. 17.

U.S. Congress, *Congressional Record,* 90th Cong., 1st Sess., 1966, 113, pt. 12.

U.S. Department of Agriculture, Bureau of Agriculture Economics. 1935. *Economic and Social Problems and Conditions of Southern Appalachia,* Miscellaneous Publication No. 205. Washington, D.C.: U.S. Government Printing Office.

U.S. Department of Agriculture, Economic Research Service. 1965. *An Economic Survey of the Appalachian Region,* Agriculture Economic Report No. 69. Washington, D.C.: U.S. Government Printing Office.

U.S. Department of Agriculture, Economic Research Service. 1966. *Rural People in the American Economy,* Economic Research Bulletin No. 101. Washington, D.C.: U.S. Government Printing Office.

U.S. Department of Agriculture, Economic Research Service. 1967.

Economics of Scale in Farming, Agriculture Economic Report No. 107. Washington, D.C.: U.S. Government Printing Office.

U.S. President, *Economic Report of the President, 1968.* Washington, D.C.: U.S. Government Printing Office.

U.S. President, *Manpower Report of the President, 1965.* Washington, D.C.: U.S. Government Printing Office.

U.S. President, *Manpower Report of the President, 1971.* Washington, D.C.: U.S. Government Printing Office.

U.S. President's National Advisory Commission on Rural Poverty. 1967. *The People Left Behind.* Washington, D.C.: U.S. Government Printing Office.

U.S. President's National Advisory Commission on Rural Poverty. 1968. *Rural Poverty in the United States.* Washington, D.C.: U.S. Government Printing Office.

Valentine, Charles A. 1968. *Culture and Poverty.* Chicago: Univ. of Chicago Press.

Wallace, T., and Hoover, M. 1966. "Income Effect of Innovation: The Case of Labor in Agriculture." *Journal of Farm Economics* 48: 325–338.

Weller. Jack E. 1966. *Yesterday's People.* Lexington: Univ. of Kentucky Press.

Wilcox, Clair. 1960. *Public Policy Toward Business.* Rev. ed. Homewood, Ill.: Richard D. Irwin.

Young, Virginia H. 1970. "Family and Childhood in a Southern Negro Community." *American Anthropologist* 72: 269–288.

Index

About the Author

Arthur M. Ford received his Ph.D. in economics from the New School for Social Research. He is presently Assistant Professor in the Department of Economics at Southern Illinois University. Professor Ford's fields of interest include political economics and economic development. He has co-edited with Robert L. Heilbroner a reader entitled *Is Economics Relevant?*